Dear Santa
Here are some
cookies for you.
I made them myself.
Merry X-mas ♥ Thea

best.

chips outside

with soft, chewy centers.

Even our children like cookies with more flavor.

Sugar

I love them bone dry, loud and

ALICE MEDRICH'S

# Cookies and Brownies

Also by Alice Medrich
*Cocolat: Extraordinary Chocolate Desserts*
*Chocolate and the Art of Low-Fat Desserts*

Warner Books, Inc.,
1271 Avenue of the Americas,
New York, NY 10020

Visit our Web site at www.warnerbooks.com

Ⓦ A Time Warner Company

Printed in the United States of America
First Printing: October 1999
10 9 8 7 6 5 4 3 2 1

Library of Congress Cataloging-in-Publication Data
Medrich, Alice.
  Alice Medrich's cookies and brownies \ Alice Medrich.
    p. cm.
  ISBN 0-446-52382-8
  1. Cookies. 2. Brownies (Cookery) I. Title.
TX772.M43 1999
641.8'654—dc21         99-11794
                  CIP

ALICE MEDRICH'S

# Cookies and Brownies

Photography
Michael Lamotte

Stylist
Sara Slavin

Design
Jacqueline Jones Design

Illustration
Kelly Burke

**WARNER BOOKS**

A Time Warner Company

**To Lucy with love**

**Acknowledgments**

My warmest thanks to Maya Klein for testing and experimenting, keeping the pace, and thinking outside the box. A hug to my agent and friend, Jane Dystel. Many thanks to my editor, Caryn Karmatz Rudy, and Harvey-Jane Kowal at Warner Books, Jackie Jones and Kristen Jester at Jacqueline Jones Design, photographer Michael Lamotte and Bill Checkvala at the Michael Lamotte Studio, stylist Sara Slavin, illustrator Kelly Burke, copy editor Susan Derecskey, and to Steve Klein for his brownie "ritual." It is a great privilege, and great fun, to work with friends.

# Contents

Acknowledgments 4

Introduction 6

Details Make a Difference 8

Techniques 12

Decorating Cookies 14

Sandwich Cookies 19

Ingredients 110

Equipment 113

Resources 115

Index 116

Shortbread 22

Butter Cookies 28

Chocolate Cookies 44

Cookie Classics 60

Biscotti 80

Brownies and Bars 90

# Introduction

Years ago I hosted a holiday cookie exchange in my home. Thirty foodies came bearing decorative tins, covered plates, and pretty baskets of home-made cookies complete with recipes. I expected a bonanza of fabulous and irresistible cookies.

What I got were overbaked cookies and underbaked cookies. Some were overbaked at the edges and underbaked in the middle. I tasted soggy cookies, tough cookies, tasteless doughy cookies, and rich cookies that were not flavorful or interesting enough to warrant the calories. Some chocolate cookies were too sweet and some were not very chocolatey. Textures were tedious, flavors were flat. I wept to see lace cookies limp and chewy instead of crisp and caramelized.

I concluded two things. First, contemporary tastes and standards for food have changed. We are exposed to better food in restaurants and at home. Also, ethnic cuisines have had a profound influence on American cooking so we appreciate, even crave, more and bigger flavors than our parents and grandparents. We want better cookies!

It's simply not enough for a cookie to be sweet and rich—we want superb texture and lots of flavor. Second, I'm convinced that cookie recipes deceive us by their simplicity. Have you ever wondered why ten people who swear by the same recipe for chocolate chip cookies produce ten startlingly different cookies, proving only that chocolate chips can make almost any lump of dough taste good? There is a myriad of uncommunicated details in the simplest cookie recipe—nothing tricky or hard to understand or execute mind you, but hidden details that can make a difference between fabulous cookies and miniature doorstops.

So my quest became to find or create recipes that satisfy a craving for heightened flavors and great textures and to communicate the details that make a difference between tough and tender, buttery versus greasy, chewy versus crisp, perfectly baked versus underbaked or overbaked, flavorful versus flat, crisp versus limp—so that ten people might produce the same good cookies using the same recipe!

"It's simply not enough for a cookie to be sweet and rich— we want superb texture and lots of flavor."

This is a small personal cookie collection rather than an encyclopedia. These are cookies that I make and serve again and again. They are simple and unfussy, rarely filled, frosted, or decorated. Just good cookies.

You will find a disproportionate number of chocolate cookies because I love chocolate, and brownies that range from very chocolatey to exceedingly chocolatey. You will find rich short-breads that are exquisitely tender and crunchy and only very lightly sweetened; butter cookies that are very buttery but not greasy; ginger cookies that are really gingery; peanut butter cookies with lots of peanut flavor; very lemony lemon cookies and luscious lemon bars. There are more crisp and crunchy than chewy cookies but even the latter have satisfying crunchy or crispy exteriors. I like interesting, noisy textures, combinations of tex-tures, and big unambiguous flavors. If a cookie is very rich, I want enough flavor and texture to feel that it's worth the fat and calories. Apropos, you will also find a few great favorites with reduced fat, and for the café crowd, a biscotti for every palate.

But no matter what your taste, you will find in these pages cookies that are easy to make and simply delicious. Let the cookie celebration begin.

# Details Make a Difference

In baking as in life, the simplest things make the biggest difference. Art requires craft, and creativity flourishes in the presence of knowledge. I want your cookies to be as sublimely flavorful, tender, and delicious as mine are when they come from my oven. To that end read about the details that make the difference.

### Try a Little Tenderness

In cookie recipes, powdered sugar in place of granulated, and cornstarch, potato starch, or rice flour substituted for a portion of the flour are often touted as magic ingredients that make cookies tender. But these starches detract from the clean bright flavor of cookies even more than they enhance the texture. And I don't like the way the starch feels on my palate. You will not find much starch or powdered sugar in this book.

**The best tender cookies are produced with good technique—proper mixing and handling.**
Tough cookies are caused by badly measured flour, the wrong kind of flour (bread flour or whole grain flours rather than all-purpose flour), too much mixing after the flour has been added to the moist ingredients in the batter, too much kneading and rerolling of scraps, or too much flour used to keep the dough from sticking to the rolling pin or the counter top. In addition, tough cookies may result from baking at too high or too low a temperature or for too long.

The fix for tough cookies is simple: Use bleached all-purpose flour, measure it accurately, mix it just enough, avoid excessive rerolling, roll out between sheets of wax paper or plastic, and check your oven and timer. You may also increase tenderness with a finer granulation of sugar, either by using superfine sugar or processing regular sugar to a finer consistency.

### Measurement Matters

Inaccurate measurements do not always spoil the cookies. You may use a liberal hand with raisins, nuts, chocolate chips, coconut, or even vanilla. Feel free to substitute dried fruits and nuts one for another and to experiment with extracts and flavors. That's the creative fun of baking.

For perfect cookies, though, you must measure the baking soda, baking powder, salt, and, most of all, flour, *carefully*. Baking is not as forgiving as general cooking, even and especially when it comes to something as simple as a cookie. If your cookies are tough, dry, doughy, or leaden, chances are your flour measurement was inaccurate.

A cup of carefully sifted all-purpose flour weighs 4 ounces, but if you pack unsifted flour firmly into that cup, it will hold 6 ounces, 50 percent more! With that margin of error, it's no wonder ten people following the same recipe can't make the same cookies.

## How to Measure Flour for the Recipes in this Book

When the recipe says "1 cup all-purpose flour," this means one cup of all-purpose flour measured without sifting. (Ignore the "pre-sifted" label on flour sacks. Presifting can eliminate stones and foreign matter, but it cannot prevent the flour from compacting again en route to your grocer's shelf.) Stir the flour in the sack or canister with a spoon if it is compacted. Spoon the flour lightly into a one-cup dry measure until it is heaped above the rim. Do not shake or tap the cup to settle the flour. Sweep a straight-edged knife or spatula across the rim of the cup to level the flour. Your level cup of unsifted all-purpose flour will weigh about 5 ounces.

## Dry and Liquid Measures

Dry measures refer to measuring cups designed to measure dry ingredients, not measuring cups that have simply been wiped dry. When using dry measures, use the appropriate tools: a one-cup measure to measure one cup, a half-cup measure to measure half a cup, and so forth.

Liquid measures are designed to measure liquid ingredients. They are clear plastic or glass containers with a pouring spout and lines up the sides to indicate measurements. To measure, set the measure on the counter; you can't hold it level in the air. Pour liquid up to the appropriate mark, with your head lowered to read the measurement at eye level.

## Mixing It Up

The basic flavor and texture of any cookie is obviously determined by the type and amount of ingredients called for in the recipe. But how much and how long the ingredients are mixed also has a surprisingly significant affect on the taste and texture of the cookie. There are two critical stages of mixing.

Most recipes begin with mixing the butter with sugar. The consistency of the butter and how long and vigorously it is beaten with the sugar affects the texture and the intensity of the flavor in subtle yet wonderful ways. I find that shortbread, chocolate chip, and oatmeal cookies are best when the butter is melted completely and simply stirred with the sugar; butter cookies have a superior flavor and texture when the butter is just softened and beaten, by hand or with an electric mixer, but only until smooth and creamy; and sugar cookies are at their best if pliable butter is beaten with sugar with an electric mixer until light and fluffy.

Flour is normally added at the end of the recipe. This is the second critical mixing phase for most cookie recipes. How long and vigorously the flour is mixed into the dough has an important—and not at all subtle—affect on cookies! Once flour is added to the moist ingredients, excess mixing makes tough cookies. This is because gluten begins to develop. The goal is to blend the flour thoroughly into the dough or batter with as little mixing as possible. The trick is to be sure that the flour is first mixed thoroughly with the other dry ingredients (leavening, spices, salt, etc.) and that it is aerated and fluffed up rather than compacted and clumped, so that it will blend easily into the dough. To this end, I mix the dry ingredients together with a wire whisk, which aerates at the same time it mixes.

In order to add the flour without excessive mixing, I like to turn the mixer off (if I am using one) and add all of the flour mixture at one time, and then commence mixing at low speed. This works if your bowl is relatively tall—at least as tall as it is wide—to prevent the flour from flying out of the bowl when the mixer is turned on. Otherwise add the dry ingredients gradually enough to avoid flying flour, but without taking any more time than necessary. Or mix in the flour with a spoon or your hands. In any case, mix only long enough to blend in the flour.

If the dough is relatively stiff, as with butter or sugar cookies, scrape the dough into a mass and knead it with your hands a few times just until smooth and with any traces of dry flour incorporated.

## How Soft Is Softened Butter?

If the recipe calls for softened butter and you are mixing with an electric mixer, allow the butter to soften at room temperature (or in the microwave at 30 percent power for a few seconds at a time) until it is pliable but not completely squishy, 65° to 70°F. If you are mixing with a large spoon or rubber spatula, it is easier if the butter is softened to the consistency of mayonnaise, 75° to 80°F.

## Baking for Best Results

Preheating the oven means getting it up to temperature. This takes fifteen to twenty minutes depending on your oven.

If your cookies are baking faster or slower than the recipe suggests, your oven may not be accurate. Test the oven with an oven thermometer and compensate accordingly or have a professional calibrate and reset the dial. All of your baking will turn out better.

The recipes in this book suggest that you bake in the upper and lower thirds of the oven, reversing cookie sheets from upper to lower and front to back about halfway through the baking period so that the cookies bake evenly.

If you wish to bake only one sheet at a time, position the rack in the center of the oven and reverse the sheet from back to front halfway through the baking period.

A common rule in cookie baking: Always cool cookie sheets before putting a new batch of raw cookies on the sheet. Warm sheets start the dough melting slowly before it goes into the oven, which can cause deformed cookie shapes, too much spreading, or altered baking times.

A little known exception to the rule: If raw cookies are already formed and laid out on a parchment or foil pan liner, you may slide the liner onto a hot or warm cookie sheet so long as you put it into the oven immediately.

Take advantage of the exception to the rule to produce scads of cookies with only one oven and two cookie sheets. While cookies are baking, keep forming cookies and laying them out on parchment or foil liners spread out on the counter. When hot cookies come from the oven, slide the hot liners onto cooling racks and slide the new liners, cookies and all, onto the hot sheets and into the hot oven immediately. Baking times may be a bit shorter, but the cookies will not suffer. Repeat the performance until you drop, or all the dough is used up, whichever comes first.

If it is important that cookies from one batch all look the same, use the same type of cookie sheet for the entire batch since each type of sheet bakes a little differently. If you are baking a variety of different-size cookies from one type of dough, group cookies of similar size on each sheet so that all of the cookies will be done at the same time. Space cookies evenly on the sheet. If your cookies are larger or smaller than the recipe calls for, the baking time and yield will necessarily be different. If you make extra large cookies, leave more space between them for spreading.

## Cooling Cookies

Cookies must be thoroughly cooled before they are stacked or stored in a closed container to prevent them from becoming soggy or misshapen from trapped steam.

If you bake on parchment- or foil-lined pans, slide the liner from the hot cookie sheet onto a cooling rack, leaving the cookies attached. Or, if you have enough pans and racks, do what the professionals do: Set the hot cookie sheet itself on the rack and allow the cookies to cool on the lined pan.

"Always cool cookie sheets before putting a new batch of raw cookies on the sheet. Warm sheets start the dough melting slowly before it goes into the oven, which can cause deformed cookie shapes, too much spreading, or altered baking times."

If baking directly on the pan, use a thin, flexible metal pancake turner to transfer each cookie from the pan to cooling racks. Some cookies can be transferred from the pan immediately; others require from 1 to 2 minutes cooling on the pan before they are firm or sturdy enough to move without breaking. If the first cookie you transfer breaks or bends, wait a minute or so and try again.

### Storing Cookies

Store cooled cookies in airtight containers: tins, jars, zipper-type plastic bags, or cookie jars with tight-fitting lids. Different kinds and flavors of cookies should be stored separately or they will all taste pretty much the same and have the same texture after a day or two. Fragile cookies should be stored in wide containers where they can lie flat with parchment or wax paper between layers. If you have iced or decorated your cookies make sure that the decoration is completely dry and set before layering the cookies between sheets of wax paper. Some cookies keep a remarkably long time—how long depends on how many times a day or a week the container is opened. Butter cookies and shortbread may keep three months or more in an airtight tin. Unless indicated otherwise, the cookies and bars in this book may be frozen for at least two to three months.

Thumbprint cookies and other filled cookies may soften in storage. Fill on the day of serving if possible. Lightly sieved powdered sugar may seep into the cookie; sieve shortly before serving. Cookies rolled in powdered sugar may need a final rolling before serving. Use your judgment.

## Techniques

### Pan Preparation

The best-tasting oatmeal or chocolate chip cookies —with deliciously caramelized crisp edges and moist chewy centers—are baked directly on the pan or on a pan lined with aluminum foil. By contrast, meringue cookies and chocolate cookies benefit from the slight insulation provided by a parchment paper liner, which results in a slower, more even bake. Some of the dark-colored, reusable nonstick pan liners seem to keep cookies relatively soft, which is why I do not use them. Consult each recipe for pan preparation.

### Chilling and Resting the Dough

Cookies are so simple to make that it seems a shame to deny the convenience, not to mention the instant gratification, of mixing and baking on the spur of the moment. Many cookie doughs, however, improve with at least two hours of chilling, preferably overnight. It is the time, rather than the temperature, which makes the difference. The moisture in the dough is absorbed by the dry ingredients and dissolves some of the sugar. This causes extra caramelization (browning), which improves flavor. After chilling, flavors are noticeably more developed and better integrated, and some cookies are both more tender and crisper. Even the appearance of some cookies is enhanced by chilling: Cookies spread less on the pan and some develop an appetizing sheen on the surface.

Nuts, chocolate chips, and other additions often poke through the dough and show themselves off more after chilling.

Chilled cookie dough is usually too stiff to form drop cookies easily with a spoon. Let it soften at room temperature. A cookie or portion scoop is easier to use than a spoon.

If you must cheat on the chilling period, your results will be tasty and acceptable anyway (although cutout cookies do not hold a good shape unless chilled). But if just once you compare cookies mixed and baked immediately with cookies baked after an overnight chill, you will change your cookie-making habits forever. Keep cookie dough on hand in the freezer to satisfy spur-of-the-moment desires or choose recipes that do not recommend a chilling period.

### Rolling and Cutting Cookies

Traditionally, cookie dough is rolled out on a well-floured board with a floured rolling pin and lots of flour sprinkled everywhere to prevent it from sticking. All that excess flour tends to toughen the cookies and the procedure is tricky for inexperienced bakers anyway. A better, easier, and less messy technique is to roll the dough between sheets of wax paper or, better yet, a cut-apart plastic bag.

Cookie dough contains enough butter and sugar to ensure that it softens quickly once it comes out of the refrigerator. For this reason I usually work with half of the dough at a time. Form and wrap the dough into two flattened patties and refrigerate until needed.

Remove one patty from the refrigerator and let it sit at room temperature until supple enough to roll but still quite firm. It will continue to soften as you work. Roll the dough to the required thickness between two pieces of wax paper or between heavy plastic sheets from a plastic bag. Turn over the dough between the sheets once or twice while you are rolling it out to check for deep wrinkles, and, if necessary, peel off and smooth the paper over the dough before continuing to roll it. When the dough is thin enough, peel off the top sheet of paper or plastic and keep it in front of you. Invert the dough onto that sheet and peel off the second sheet. Cut cookie shapes as close together as possible to minimize scraps, dipping the edges of cookie cutters in flour as necessary to prevent sticking. Use the point of a paring knife

"Chilled cookie dough is usually too stiff to form drop cookies easily with a spoon. Let it soften at room temperature."

to lift and remove scraps as you transfer cookies to baking sheets. If the dough gets too soft at any time—while rolling, cutting, removing scraps between cookies, or transferring cookies—slide a cookie sheet underneath the bottom sheet of paper or plastic and refrigerate the dough for a few minutes until firm. Repeat with the second piece of dough. Press all of the dough scraps together gently (don't overwork them with too much kneading) and reroll.

### Scooping and Shaping Cookies

Cookies bake more evenly if they are all the same size. A cookie scoop (also called portion scoop) with a squeeze-release handle is the best tool for forming equal-size lumps of cookie dough quickly and easily, whether the dough is relatively firm or soft and gooey. Slightly more than a level tablespoon of dough (#60 portion scoop) will form a ball 1 1/4 inches in diameter; use two level teaspoons of dough (#100 scoop) to form a 1-inch ball.

To portion firm or chilled dough without a cookie scoop, shape the dough into a neat square patty about 3/4 inch thick before it is chilled. Cut the chilled patty into equal squares; for a yield of three dozen cookies, cut a six-by-six grid. Shape each piece into a ball, or a crescent, or what you will.

## Decorating Cookies

### Impressions

Butter cookie dough (see page 31) can be imprinted, scored, or marked before baking with cookie stamps or ordinary household or kitchen objects such as meat-tenderizing mallets, forks, graters, kids' toys, and other found objects. For deep impressions, form the dough into a ball, then press with the chosen imprinter until the cookie is as thin as desired. Test the imprinter to see if it sticks to the cookie dough; grease and/or dust it with flour if necessary. For the best impressions, refrigerate imprinted cookies for at least 30 minutes before baking.

### Piping

For piped cookie decorations that dry hard and taste good too, nothing beats melted chocolate. It's simple to use (although it must be kept warm) and requires no tempering. Use white chocolate, milk chocolate, or dark chocolate; use bars, rather than chocolate chips, which do not melt well. Pipe on cookies after they have baked and cooled.

### Melted Chocolate

Chop 3 ounces of chocolate (dark chocolate, milk chocolate, or white chocolate) into small pieces and place it in a clean dry heatproof bowl. Fill a wide shallow pan or skillet with about 1 inch of water and bring it to a gentle simmer.

To melt semisweet or bittersweet chocolate, set the bowl of chocolate in the skillet and stir constantly until melted and smooth. (Or microwave on medium power for 2 to 2¹/₂ minutes, stirring from time to time, just until the chocolate is melted and smooth.)

To melt white chocolate or milk chocolate, remove the simmering skillet from the heat and wait 30 seconds before setting the bowl of chocolate in it. Stir constantly until the chocolate is melted and smooth. (Or microwave on low for 2 to 2¹/₂ minutes, stirring from time to time, until the chocolate is melted and smooth.) Scrape the chocolate into a small disposable parchment paper cone or plastic decorating bag, or the corner of a zipper-type plastic bag. Close the bag and snip off a tip. Pipe the chocolate onto the cookies. Let set and harden before storing between layers of wax paper. If the chocolate begins to harden in the cone or bag, microwave on low power for 10 seconds at a time until the chocolate is warm and flowing again.

If a color other than white, tan, or dark brown is wanted, tint white chocolate with oil-based or powdered food colorings (see page 115) designed especially for the purpose. Ordinary food coloring, which is water based, is incompatible with chocolate.

**Easy Cookie Icing**

Easy Cookie Icing, plain white or tinted with ordinary food colors, is an easy, though less flavorful, alternative to melted chocolate. Spread it with a small spatula, paint it with a brush, or pipe it from a parchment paper cone or the corner of a zipper-type plastic bag (fill it, close it, and snip off a tip). Powdered sugar dissolved in just a little liquid dries hard and shiny and takes color well. It is sweet and decorative, not a gourmet item.

**How to Make Easy Cookie Icing**

For 1 cup of icing, mix 4 cups powdered sugar with 3 to 4 tablespoons water, or lemon juice (for a lemon-flavored icing), or 5 to 6 tablespoons brandy or rum to the desired consistency. Adjust by adding powdered sugar or liquid. If desired, divide the icing among small cups and tint with ordinary food coloring. Note that food coloring intensifies with time, so tint the icing lighter than you think it should be. To store, press plastic wrap against the surface of the icing. Icing keeps about 4 days at room temperature.

**Flocking and Beading**

Here's a controlled but creative way of decorating cookies with colored sugar decorations, which is more interesting than random sprinkling. Pipe melted chocolate (white chocolate is especially good if you are going to flock with

"Lots of special effects and details are possible for decorating cookie dolls, fancy party favors, Christmas tree ornaments, or any other show-off cookies, where each cookie is a unique work of art."

colored material) onto the cookies, then use it like glue to affix sprinkles and candies. Lots of special effects and details are possible for decorating cookie dolls, fancy party favors, Christmas tree ornaments, or any other show-off cookies, where each cookie is a unique work of art.

Gather an assortment of decorations: colored sprinkles, sugars, jimmies, or other very tiny decorations. Pour a generous amount of each into a shallow plate or saucer at least as big as the cookies you will decorate. Place larger decorations like miniature M&Ms, jelly beans, and silver shot into little cups.

Prepare melted chocolate (see page 17) or cookie icing (see page 15) and scrape it into a parchment paper cone or the corner of a zipper-type plastic bag. Snip the tip of the cone or bag with scissors so that you can squeeze the chocolate or icing in a controllable thin line.

Pipe decorative lines, shapes, or borders with chocolate or icing wherever you want to affix a particular type of sprinkle, then press the cookie gently, piping side down, into the plate of sprinkles. Set the cookie aside to dry. To add a second type of sprinkle to the same cookie, pipe fresh lines on the cookie and dip into another plate. Continue as desired. Embed larger decorations in chocolate or icing by hand, one by one. Let decorations dry completely before storing cookies between layers of wax paper or sliding each into a cellophane bag.

### Gold and Silver Powder (Petal Dust)

Gold powder and silver powder, also called petal dust or lustre dust, can be applied directly to cookies with a tiny brush. Or the powder can be dissolved in vodka and applied like paint. Dissolve 1/2 teaspoon of powder by adding vodka one drop at a time, stirring with a tiny brush, until it is the consistency of paint. Add a drop of vodka as necessary as it evaporates.

### Dipping Cookies in Chocolate

Cookies half dipped in fine chocolate are festive and fancy. The chocolate must be melted and tempered so that it will dry hard and shiny instead of gray and streaky on the cookies. Biscotti (pages 80–89) and Basic Butter Cookies (page 31) are grand dipped in chocolate. Coconut Macaroons (page 62) and Almond Macaroons (page 64) are superb dipped in semisweet or bittersweet chocolate. Brown Sugar Butter Cookies (page 32) and Butter Pecan Cookies made with brown sugar (page 32) go well with white chocolate. You will need: cookies, baked, cooled, and at room temperature; cookie sheets lined with wax paper; and tempered chocolate. Have the baked and cooled cookies ready and at room temperature before tempering, as well as cookie sheets lined with wax paper to set the cookies on after dipping.

Hold a cookie with your thumb on the top of the cookie and forefinger on the bottom. Dip the cookie half to two thirds of the way into the tempered chocolate. Shake the cookie, letting the excess chocolate flow back into the container.

Wipe some of the chocolate gently off the bottom of the cookie against the edge of the chocolate bowl. Set the cookie, right side up, on the lined cookie sheet. When you have filled a whole sheet with dipped cookies, refrigerate them for five minutes to set the chocolate. Remove the cookies from the refrigerator and let them sit in a cool place until the chocolate is completely hardened and cookies come cleanly off the wax paper. Store cookies between sheets of wax paper in an airtight container at cool room temperature.

### Tempered Chocolate for Dipping Cookies

Tempering chocolate involves a sequence of heating, stirring, and cooling steps that stabilize the cocoa butter (fat) crystals and ensure that the chocolate dries hard and shiny. This tempering method works only if it is followed rigorously. You must start with a fresh new bar of solid chocolate: It was tempered by the manufacturer and is still in temper as long as it still looks glossy rather than gray or dull when you unwrap it. The trick is to melt the tempered chocolate so gently that the temper in the bar is not destroyed. This method cannot be used to temper chocolate that is already out of temper, having been melted to an unknown temperature, or that looks dull, mottled, or gray.

### How to Temper Chocolate

Choose good-tasting chocolate. Do not use chocolate chips or chocolate coatings, which are not truly chocolate. Do not work in a hot room. Do not allow any moisture to come in direct contact with the chocolate. Resist the temptation to hurry the process with extra heat, and don't be too lazy to chop the chocolate as finely as directed. Make sure that the inside of the bowl, the spatula, and the thermometer stem are clean and dry. Whenever you take the temperature of the chocolate or the water, wipe the stem clean and dry with a piece of paper towel.

*Makes enough to dip about 48*
*2 1/2- to 3-inch cookies*

### Ingredients

1 pound semisweet, bittersweet, milk, or
   white chocolate
4 ounces extra chocolate, in 1 or 2 chunks

### Equipment

Heatproof glass bowl with a 2 1/2- to 3-quart capacity
Instant-read thermometer
Rubber spatula
Roasting pan or large baking pan at least
   2 inches deep

Cut the pound of chocolate into pieces the size and shape of matchsticks or chop it into small pebble-shape pieces no larger than peas (this can be done in batches in a food processor). Put the chocolate in the bowl and set the bowl in the roasting pan. Set the extra chocolate chunks aside. Pour hot tap water (120° to 130°F.) into the roasting pan until it reaches just above the level of the chocolate in the bowl. Let sit for 5 to 6 minutes, or until the chocolate around the sides of the bowl is partially melted. Stir with the rubber spatula until the chocolate pieces are all sticky and are beginning to clump together. There will be barely enough melted chocolate to accomplish this. Remove the bowl and empty the water from the roasting pan. Replace the bowl of chocolate in the roasting pan and replenish with hot tap water. Let sit for 2 to 3 minutes. Begin stirring with the rubber spatula, turning the sticky mass over and over. Keep stirring (it may take 5 minutes), spreading the chocolate against the sides of the warm bowl and scraping it off as it melts. Do not replenish the hot water; it is still warm enough to do the job. When about three quarters of the chocolate is melted, check its temperature. If it is less than its maximum temperature of 90°F. for dark chocolate (88°F. for milk chocolate or white chocolate), continue to stir. Remove the bowl from the warm water as soon as the chocolate reaches the maximum temperature, even if it is not entirely melted. Wipe the outside of the bowl dry. Stir the chocolate thoroughly for at least 30 seconds, to equalize the temperature and melt any remaining pieces. The chocolate is now melted and still in temper. Use it for dipping immediately.

If you accidentally exceed the maximum temperature, even by only a couple of degrees, the chocolate will probably be out of temper. Keep the bowl out of the roasting pan. Add the reserved chocolate chunks and stir until the temperature of the melted chocolate falls below the maximum (90°F. for dark chocolate, 88°F. for milk chocolate or white chocolate). The chunks will not be entirely melted, but the chocolate may be back in temper.

To test it, smear a dab of chocolate, 1/16-inch thick, on a small piece of wax paper and put it in a cool place in the room or in the refrigerator. If the smear begins to dry and set within 5 minutes in a cool place or 3 minutes in the refrigerator, it is back in temper. Remove the chunks and refrigerate for 10 minutes, then reserve for reuse. Stir the chocolate thoroughly before dipping. If the smear still looks wet and shiny, continue to stir the chunks of chocolate in the bowl for 2 to 3 minutes more and test again. Repeat until the chocolate is in temper.

Stir tempered chocolate from time to time as you work with it. If it cools or thickens too much, set the bowl in a pan of water only 2 degrees warmer than the maximum temperature for the chocolate (above), and stir until the chocolate is rewarmed. The chocolate will remain in temper so long as you do not let it exceed its maximum temperature.

# Sandwich Cookies

The best sandwich cookies I know are the simplest—filled with Chocolate Ganache (page 21), Peanut Filling (page 20), or Lemon Curd (page 20). For dainty sandwiches roll cookies a little thinner than usual. Or fill cookies with jams and preserves, Melted Chocolate (page 14), Nutella (chocolate-hazelnut spread), or ice cream.

Cookies filled with jam or preserves soften quickly because of the moisture in the jams, so it's best to fill the cookies very shortly before serving. Basic Butter Cookies (page 31) and Linzer Cookies (page 37) are excellent with jam. Try Espresso Walnut Cookies (page 35), substituting any nut you like and omitting the espresso powder. Pair blackberry preserves with walnut or toasted hazelnut cookies, raspberry or apricot preserves or citrus marmalade with almond cookies, strawberry preserves with peanut cookies, pineapple or guava preserves with macadamia cookies, and so forth. Use 1 teaspoon of jam for each sandwich; 1 cup of jam fills about forty-eight $2^{1}/_{2}$- to 3-inch sandwich cookies.

For chocolate-filled sandwiches, choose good eating quality chocolate rather than chocolate chips. I like Vanilla Sugar Cookies (page 33) and Basic Butter Cookies (or nut variations) (page 31) filled with bittersweet or semisweet chocolate, Brown Sugar Cookies (page 32) and Butter Pecan Cookies (page 32) with white chocolate, and

Mexican Chocolate Wafers or Chocolate Espresso Wafers filled with milk chocolate.

Spread 1 to 1 1/2 teaspoons Melted Chocolate —no tempering is necessary—between two 2 1/2- to 3-inch cookies sandwiched back to back. Let cookies sit at room temperature or refrigerate briefly to harden the chocolate. Six ounces of chocolate fills about twenty-four 2 1/2- to 3-inch sandwich cookies.

Vanilla ice cream is a sublime filling for Chocolate Chip Cookies (page 48), Double Chocolate Chip Cookies (page 50), Oatmeal Cookies (page 75), Ginger Snaps (page 79)—use your imagination. Soften the ice cream in the refrigerator, not at room temperature, just until it is soft enough to scoop and press between cookies without breaking them. Refreeze until serving. If the sandwiches are rock hard, let them soften briefly before serving. Count on about 3 tablespoons of ice cream for a 3-inch cookie. One pint fills about 10 sandwiches.

### Lemon Curd

Fill cookies shortly before serving to prevent cookies from softening. Basic Butter Cookies (page 31), Vanilla Sugar Cookies (page 33), Espresso Walnut Cookies made without the espresso (page 35), and Lemon Wafers (page 69) are all excellent filled with Lemon Curd. This recipe makes enough to fill up to 80 sandwich cookies or 250 thumbprints. Don't forget that leftover Lemon Curd is delicious on toast or scones.

*Makes 1 3/4 cups*

### Ingredients
3 large eggs
1/2 cup strained fresh lemon juice
Grated zest of 1 lemon
1/2 cup sugar
6 tablespoons unsalted butter, cut into pieces

Whisk the eggs lightly in a medium heatproof bowl, to combine yolks and whites. Combine the lemon juice, zest, sugar, and butter in a small nonreactive saucepan and heat to a simmer over medium heat. Pour the hot liquid gradually over the eggs, whisking constantly until all the liquid has been combined with the eggs. Return the mixture to the saucepan and whisk over medium heat until thickened and just beginning to simmer around the edges. Remove from the heat and strain the mixture into a clean container, pressing gently on the solids. Refrigerate before using. Spread 1 to 1 1/2 teaspoons of Lemon Curd between two 2 1/2- to 3-inch cookies or pipe into thumbprint cookies. *Lemon Curd may be prepared, covered, and refrigerated for up to 1 week.*

### Peanut Filling

Brown Sugar Butter Cookies (page 32) and Vanilla Sugar Cookies (page 33) make delicious peanut butter sandwich cookies. Use this filling for thumbprints as well. For a smooth filling, or if you plan to pipe the filling, use smooth peanut butter and omit the chopped peanuts. I prefer the flavor of Adams and Laura Scudder's brands of natural peanut butter, made simply with peanuts and salt and without added sugar or hydrogenated fat. This recipe makes enough to fill up to 60 sandwich cookies or 192 thumbprint cookies.

*Makes about 1 1/3 cups*

### Ingredients
6 tablespoons unsalted butter, softened
1 cup powdered sugar (3/4 cup if not using natural
  unsweetened peanut butter)
2/3 cup natural nutty or smooth peanut butter
1/4 cup roasted unsalted peanuts, chopped
  medium fine (optional)

Beat the butter with the powdered sugar just until smooth. Mix in the peanut butter and chopped peanuts, if using. Spread 1 to 1 1/2 teaspoons of filling between two 2 1/2- to 3-inch cookies, or pipe into thumbprint cookies. *Filling may be covered and refrigerated for several weeks.*

### Chocolate Ganache
Decadent chocolate cream to fill sandwich cookies, Peanut Butter Thumbprints (page 73), or Nutty Thumbprint Cookies (page 42). Use a good-quality chocolate for this world-class filling, rather than chocolate chips. This recipe makes enough for about 48 sandwich cookies or about 200 thumbprint cookies. Leftover ganache can be melted and used to top ice cream.

*Makes 1 1/2 cups*

### Ingredients
6 ounces semisweet or bittersweet chocolate
1 cup heavy whipping cream

Chop the chocolate into small pieces and put it in a heatproof bowl. Bring the cream to a boil in a heavy-bottomed saucepan. Pour the hot cream over the chopped chocolate. Stir gently until all of the chocolate is melted and the mixture is smooth. Cool the ganache at room temperature until it is thick enough to spread or pipe. *May be covered, stored, in the refrigerator for at least 1 week.*

To soften chilled ganache, set the bowl in a larger bowl of hot water or microwave on low for a few seconds at a time until soft and spreadable. Spread about 2 1/2 teaspoons of ganache between two 1 1/2- to 3-inch cookies or pipe into thumbprint cookies.

basic shortbread
25

chocolate shortbread
26

**e Quest for Perfect Shortbread** I tried dozens of shortbread recipes to find that my grandmother was ht once again. She didn't know a lot about this type of cookie, but she always said that "plain is best," d shortbreads are no exception. I found that all-purpose flour, unsalted butter, granulated sugar, and nilla produced the very best tasting shortbread. Recipes that included some measure of cornstarch, tato starch, or rice flour for extra tenderness or powdered sugar instead of granulated sugar just dn't measure up to my expectations for flavor or texture. Tenderness, I found, was a matter of how u handle the ingredients rather than what you substitute for them.

# Shortbread

### Here's what I learned

...For the tenderest Basic Shortbread (and variations), use melted butter; for the tenderest Chocolate Shortbread, use softened butter.

...Do not overbeat shortbread dough. A large spoon is usually better than an electric mixer.

...Grease the pan or line it with foil rather than with parchment for the evenest browning on the bottom.

...It is unnecessary to prick the dough before baking.

...For superior flavor and texture, chill the dough in the pan before baking, for at least two hours, preferably overnight.

...Shortbread looks done long before it actually is, which may tempt you to remove it from the oven too soon. Underbaked shortbread is nice and dry and crunchy at the edges and disappointingly doughy in the middle. If this happens, put all of the pieces on a cookie sheet and return them to the oven for 15 minutes at 300°F. This does the trick so well that I am tempted to bake all my shortbread twice on purpose.

The best plain shortbread is simple to make. One secret is melt
butter *(I know, I know, I didn't think it would work either)* and anoth
is making sure that the dough is chilled for at least two hours, if n
overnight, before baking. Variations follow, which will get you started o
creating your own flavors. Shortbread keeps for many weeks in
sealed container and thus makes a great do-ahead gi

# Basic Shortbread

Cut the butter into chunks and melt it in a large saucepan over medium heat. Remove from the heat and stir in the sugar, vanilla, and salt. Add the flour and mix just until incorporated. Pat and spread the dough evenly in the pan. Refrigerate for at least 2 hours or overnight.

Preheat the oven to 300°F. Position a rack in the lower third of the oven. Bake the shortbread for 65 to 75 minutes (a few minutes less if using the tart pan), or until well browned and dark brown at the edges. Remove from the oven and sprinkle with sugar. While still hot, use a thin sharp knife to cut the shortbread into wedges, oblongs, or squares. *May be stored airtight for at least 1 month.*

## Variations

**Walnut Shortbread:** Adding ground nuts to shortbread produces extraordinary flavor and melting tenderness. Try pecans, toasted and skinned hazelnuts (see page 111), toasted or untoasted almonds, peanuts, or any nut you've got a craving for.

Decrease the flour to 1 1/4 cups. Add 1/2 cup walnut pieces to the flour and pulse in a food processor until the nuts are finely ground. Proceed with the basic recipe.

**Bourbon Pecan or Peanut Shortbread:** Make Walnut Shortbread, substituting pecans or peanuts for the walnuts, substituting brown sugar for the granulated sugar, and adding 1 tablespoon bourbon with the vanilla.

**Brown Sugar Shortbread:** Substitute light or dark brown sugar for the granulated sugar, or use half brown sugar and half granulated sugar.

**Nutmeg Shortbread:** Add a scant 3/4 teaspoon freshly grated nutmeg to the flour.

**Cardamom Shortbread:** Add a scant 1/2 teaspoon ground cardamom to the flour.

kes 16 large or 32 small pieces

gredients

tablespoons unsalted butter
ablespoons sugar
easpoon vanilla extract
teaspoon salt
2 cups all-purpose flour
easpoons extra sugar, for
sprinkling after baking

quipment

inch round or 8-inch
square pan, or a 9 1/2-inch
fluted tart pan, greased or
lined with foil

Good-quality Dutch process cocoa (see page 11
has a rich mellow flavor that makes th
subtle shortbread particularly good. Softened butt
rather than melted butter, is be:

# Chocolate Shortbread

Mix the flour and cocoa together thoroughly with a whisk or fork. Set aside.

With a large spoon or an electric mixer, beat the butter with the sugar, vanilla, and salt until creamy and smooth but not at all fluffy, less than 1 minute with the electric mixer. Add the flour mixture and mix just until incorporated. Press the dough evenly in the pan. Refrigerate for at least 2 hours or overnight.

Preheat the over to 300°F. Position a rack in the lower third of the oven.

Bake shortbread for 65 to 70 minutes (a few minutes less if using the tart pan), or until firm. Remove from the oven and sprinkle with sugar. Cool for 5 to 10 minutes. Use a thin sharp knife to cut the shortbread into wedges, oblongs, or squares. *May be stored airtight for at least 1 month.*

## Variations

Mocha Shortbread: Reduce the cocoa to 2 tablespoons. Combine 4 teaspoons instant espresso powder with the vanilla before adding it to the dough.

Spicy Chocolate Shortbread: Add 1/4 teaspoon ground cinnamon, a pinch of cayenne, and a pinch of ground black pepper to the flour.

*Makes 16 large or 32 small pieces*

### Ingredients

1 1/2 cups all-purpose flour
3 tablespoons Dutch process
  cocoa
12 tablespoons unsalted butter,
  softened
6 tablespoons sugar
1 teaspoon vanilla extract
1/4 teaspoon salt
2 teaspoons extra sugar, for
  sprinkling after baking

### Equipment

9-inch round or 8-inch
  square pan, or a 9 1/2-inch
  fluted tart pan, greased or
  lined with foil

basic butter cookies
31

vanilla sugar cookies
33

espresso walnut coo
35

linzer cookies
37

mexican wedding cakes
41

snicker doodles
43

er cookies call forth a vivid childhood memory of attractive tin boxes, divided into fluted paper-lined
mpartments filled with a wonderland of pale cookies. Cookies shaped like stars and wreaths, filled with
ky jam, littered with colored sprinkles or pulverized nuts. Ever a hopeful child, I nibbled expectantly
n each compartment certain I would soon find the really good one. I did not discover how compelling,
nchy, flavorful, and divinely buttery a cookie could be until I owned a bakery of my own and began to
ate—of all things—butter cookies. I started with a plain one and dipped it in bittersweet chocolate.
rown sugar version came next, then one with espresso and walnuts, and then bourbon and pecans.
I so forth. For this book, I revisited and retested those recipes and came up with some delectable results.

# Butter Cookies

*Here's what I learned*

…The simplest, clearest flavor and crispest tender texture result from the simplest ingredients: butter, flour, sugar, and salt only. Cookies made with egg yolk are a little richer and more complex in flavor with a very delicate melt-in-your-mouth soft tenderness. (I found that adding a whole egg made the cookies crisper and sturdier but tougher.)

…The most successful additions to butter cookies are those ingredients that are compatible but do not compete with the flavor of butter: nuts, brown or maple sugars, spices, and spirits. Chocolate is less successful as an integral flavoring but very nice as a coating.

…Softened, not melted, butter, beaten only until smooth and creamy, not fluffy, produces the best flavor and texture.

…Chilling the dough for at least 2 hours, if not overnight, makes a better-tasting cookie with a more tender and crunchier crumb than baking immediately.

…Butter cookies taste best when baked on an ungreased pan; if you must line the pan use foil rather than parchment paper.

…The basic recipe bakes best at 350°F. The egg yolk variation is best baked at 325°F.

Magnificently plain, tender, crunchy cookies celebrate the taste of butter without being too rich or greasy. Have fun with the variations or dream up your own.

# asic Butter Cookies

h the back of a large spoon in a medium mixing bowl or with a mixer,
t the butter with the sugar, salt, and vanilla until smooth and creamy but
fluffy, about 1 minute with the mixer. Add the flour and mix just until
orporated. Scrape the dough into a mass and knead it with your hands a
times just until smooth.

slice-and-bake cookies, form a 12 X 2-inch log. For rolled and cut cookies,
n 2 flat patties. Wrap and refrigerate the dough for at least 2 hours,
ferably overnight. *The dough may be frozen for up to 3 months.*

heat the oven to 350°F. Position the racks in the upper and lower thirds
he oven.

slice and bake cookies: Use a sharp knife to cut the cold dough log into
es 1/4 inch thick. Place cookies at least 11/2 inches apart on cookie sheets.

roll and cut cookies: Remove 1 patty from the refrigerator and let it sit
room temperature until supple enough to roll but still quite firm. It will con-
ue to soften as you work. Roll the dough between 2 pieces of wax paper
between heavy plastic sheets from a plastic bag to a thickness of 1/4 inch.
n the dough over once or twice while you are rolling it out to check for
ep wrinkles; if necessary, peel off and smooth the paper or plastic over the
ugh before continuing to roll it. When the dough is thin enough, peel off
e top sheet of paper or plastic and keep it in front of you. Invert the dough
to that sheet and peel off the second sheet. Cut cookie shapes as close
gether as possible to minimize scraps, dipping the edges of cookie cutters in
ur as necessary to prevent sticking. Use the point of a paring knife to lift and
move scraps as you transfer cookies to cookie sheets. Place cookies at least
/2 inches apart on cookie sheets. If the dough gets too soft at any time—
hile rolling, cutting, removing scraps between cookies, or transferring cook-
s—slide a cookie sheet underneath the paper or plastic and refrigerate the
ugh for a few minutes until firm. Repeat with the second piece of dough.

*(continued)*

*Makes about 48 2-inch cookies*

### Ingredients

16 tablespoons unsalted butter,
  softened
3/4 cup sugar
1/4 teaspoon salt
1 1/2 teaspoons vanilla extract
2 cups all-purpose flour

### Equipment

2 cookie sheets, ungreased

Press all of the dough scraps together gently (don't overwork them with too much kneading), and reroll.

Bake for 12 to 14 minutes, or until light golden brown at the edges, rotating the cookie sheets from top to bottom and front to back halfway through the baking time to ensure even baking. Repeat until all the cookies are baked.

Let cookies firm up on the pan for about 1 minute before transferring them to a rack with a metal pancake turner. Cool completely before stacking or storing. Cookies are delicious fresh but even better the next day. *May be stored airtight, for at least 1 month.*

**Variations**

**Basic Butter Cookies with Egg:** Preheat the oven to 325°F. (instead of 350°F.). Mix 1 large egg yolk into the butter mixture before adding the flour. Bake on an ungreased pan about 16 to 18 minutes, or until lightly colored at the edges.

**Eggnog Cookies:** Prepare Basic Butter Cookies with Egg, adding 4 teaspoons of rum or brandy and 1/4 teaspoon freshly grated (or ground) nutmeg with the vanilla.

**Brown Sugar or Maple Butter Cookies with or without Nuts:** Brown sugar imparts a rich butterscotch flavor, while maple sugar is more delicate. Both of these cookies may soften a little if stored longer than a week.

Substitute light or dark brown sugar or maple granules (granulated maple sugar available from some specialty and natural food stores and by mail order) for the sugar. If using maple granules, omit the vanilla extract. If desired, mix 1 cup chopped walnuts or pecans into the dough after the flour.

**Butter Pecan Cookies:** Spread 1 cup pecan halves on a cookie sheet and toast them at 325°F. for 7 to 9 minutes, or until fragrant and lightly colored. Cool and chop the nuts. Prepare Basic Butter Cookies adding 4 teaspoons of bourbon with the vanilla. Mix in the pecans after the flour.

Since preschool, my daughter, Lucy, and I have celebrated
her February birthday by making sugar cookie hearts
for her classmates. Each cookie is a unique work of art,
decorated with a child's name and a fancy border piped in
melted chocolate and studded with colorful sugar.

# anilla Sugar Cookies

mbine the flour, baking powder, and salt in a bowl and mix together
roughly with a whisk or a fork. Set aside.

at the butter and sugar in a large bowl with an electric mixer until light and
ffy, 3 to 4 minutes. Beat in the eggs and vanilla. On low speed, beat in the
ur just until incorporated. Scrape the dough into a mass and knead it with
ur hands a few times until smooth. Divide the dough into 4 pieces and
m each into a flat patty. Wrap and refrigerate the patties until firm enough
roll, preferably several hours or overnight.

eheat the oven to 350°F. Position the racks in the upper and lower thirds
the oven.

roll and cut cookies: Remove 1 patty from the refrigerator and let it sit
room temperature until supple enough to roll but still quite firm. It will con-
ue to soften as you work. Roll the dough between 2 pieces of wax paper
between heavy plastic sheets from a plastic bag to a thickness of $1/8$ inch.
rn the dough over once or twice while you are rolling it out to check for
ep wrinkles; if necessary, peel off and smooth the paper over the dough
fore continuing to roll it. When the dough is thin enough, peel off the top
eet of paper or plastic and keep it in front of you. Invert the dough onto

*Makes about 90 2 1/2- inch cookies
or 55 3 1/2- inch cookies*

**Ingredients**

3 3/4 cups all-purpose flour
1 teaspoon baking powder
1/2 teaspoon salt
16 tablespoons unsalted butter,
   slightly softened
2 cups sugar
2 large eggs
1 tablespoon vanilla extract

**Equipment**

2 cookie sheets, lined with foil
   or greased

*(continued)*

*Our passion for cookie decorating reached new heights when we began cutting out shapely eight-inch fashion-doll cookies and dressing them in ball gowns or bikinis beaded with miniature M&Ms and swanky silver shot. Mink stoles are made of chocolate jimmies, and gaudy jelly-bean jewelry is de rigueur. I have seen a kitchen full of little girls (and some old ones too) enthralled for hours designing cookie couture.*

that sheet and peel off the second sheet. Cut cookie shapes as close together as possible to minimize scraps, dipping the edges of cookie cutters in flour as necessary to prevent sticking. Use the point of a paring knife to lift and remove scraps as you transfer cookies to cookie sheets. Place cookies at least 1 1/2 inches apart on the cookie sheets. If the dough gets too soft at any time—while rolling, cutting, removing scraps between cookies, or transferring cookies—slide a cookie sheet underneath the paper or plastic and refrigerate the dough for a few minutes until firm. Repeat with the remaining pieces of dough. Press all of the dough scraps together gently (don't overwork them with too much kneading), and reroll.

Bake for 8 to 10 minutes, or until pale golden at the edges, rotating the cookie sheets from top to bottom and front to back halfway through the baking time to ensure even baking. Repeat until all the cookies are baked.

Slide parchment liners onto cooling racks or transfer the cookies directly from the pan to the rack with a metal pancake turner, waiting 1 or 2 minutes if necessary to let cookies firm up before moving them. Cool cookies completely before stacking, decorating, or storing. *May be kept, airtight, for at least 1 month.*

These are adult cookies—not too sweet, and distinctly coffee flavored. Serve with a dish of coffee ice cream and a cup of coffee. To vary the recipe, omit the espresso powder and coffee bean garnish and substitute any other nut for the walnuts.

# spresso Walnut Cookies

x the espresso powder with the brandy and vanilla in a small cup. t aside.

mbine the flour, walnuts, sugar, and salt in the bowl of a food processor ed with a steel blade. Pulse until the walnuts are finely ground. Add the tter (cut into several pieces if firm). Pulse until the mixture looks damp and mbly. Drizzle in the espresso mixture and pulse until the mixture begins clump up around the blade. Remove the dough, press it into a ball, and ead it a few times to complete the mixing.

r slice-and-bake cookies, form a 12 X 2-inch log. For rolled and cut cookies, m 2 flat patties. Wrap and refrigerate the dough for at least 2 hours, eferably overnight, or up to 3 days. *The dough may be frozen for up to months.*

eheat the oven to 350°F. Position the racks in the upper and lower thirds the oven.

slice and bake cookies: Use a sharp knife to cut the cold dough log into ces 1/4 inch thick. Place cookies at least 1 1/2 inches apart on cookie sheets. ess a coffee bean in the center of each cookie.

*(continued)*

*Makes about 45 2-inch cookies*

### Ingredients

2 1/2 teaspoons instant espresso powder

1 tablespoon plus 1 teaspoon brandy

1 1/2 teaspoons vanilla extract

2 cups all-purpose flour

1 cup walnut pieces

3/4 cup sugar

1/4 teaspoon salt

16 tablespoons unsalted butter, soft or firm

45 roasted coffee or espresso beans (optional)

### Equipment

Food processor
2 cookie sheets, ungreased

To roll and cut cookies: Remove 1 patty from the refrigerator and let it sit at room temperature until supple enough to roll but still quite firm. It will contin to soften as you work. Roll the dough between 2 pieces of wax paper or between heavy plastic sheets from a plastic bag to a thickness of 1/4 inch. T the dough over once or twice while you are rolling it out to check for deep wrinkles; if necessary, peel off and smooth the paper or plastic over the dou before continuing to roll it. When the dough is thin enough, peel off the top sheet of paper or plastic and keep it in front of you. Invert the dough onto th sheet and peel off the second sheet.

Cut cookie shapes as close together as possible to minimize scraps, dipping the edges of cookie cutters in flour as necessary to prevent sticking. Use th point of a paring knife to lift and remove scraps as you transfer cookies to cookie sheets. Place cookies at least 1 1/2 inches apart on the cookie sheets. Press a coffee bean in the center of each cookie. If the dough gets too soft at any time—while rolling, cutting, removing scraps between cookies, or tran ferring cookies—slide a cookie sheet underneath the paper or plastic and refrigerate the dough for a few minutes until firm. Repeat with the second piece of dough. Press all of the dough scraps together gently (don't overwor them with too much kneading), and reroll.

Bake for 12 to 14 minutes, or until light golden brown at the edges, rotating the cookie sheets from top to bottom and front to back halfway through the baking time to ensure even baking. Repeat until all the cookies are baked.

Let cookies firm up on the pan for about 1 minute before transferring them t a rack with a metal pancake turner. Cool cookies completely before stacking or storing. Cookies are delicious fresh but even better the next day. *May be stored, airtight, for 1 month or more.*

Hearts or stars, or pretty autumn leaves—
use your imagination with shapes and try
different kinds of preserves. Personal favorites
are blackberry, raspberry, and apricot.
My version of these pretty sandwich cookies
borrows flavors from the traditional
Linzer torte: almonds and/or hazelnuts with
cinnamon, clove, and a touch of citrus.

# Linzer Cookies

Combine the flour, nuts, granulated sugar, salt, cinnamon, and cloves in the bowl of a food processor fitted with a steel blade. Pulse until the nuts are finely ground. Add the butter (cut into several pieces if firm). Pulse until the mixture looks damp and crumbly. Add the almond extract and the lemon and orange zests or extracts and pulse until the mixture begins to clump up around the blade. Remove the dough, press it into a ball, and knead it a few times to complete the mixing.

Form the dough into 2 flat patties. Wrap and refrigerate the dough for at least 2 hours, preferably overnight, or up to 3 days. *The dough may be frozen for up to 3 months.*

Preheat the oven to 325°F. Position the racks in the upper and lower thirds of the oven.

(continued)

es about 20 3 1/2- inch cookies

redients

ps all-purpose flour
up almonds and/or hazelnuts
up granulated sugar
easpoon salt
teaspoons ground
innamon
easpoon ground cloves
ablespoons unsalted butter
easpoon almond extract
aspoon grated lemon zest
r 1/4 teaspoon lemon extract
not oil)
easpoon grated orange zest
r 1/4 teaspoon orange extract
not oil)
ained or puréed good-quality
preserves or fruit spread
wdered sugar, for dusting

uipment

od processor
large and a small cookie
cutter of the same or a
different shape, for example
a 4-inch leaf and a 2-inch leaf
cookie sheets, ungreased

To roll and cut cookies: Remove 1 patty from the refrigerator and let it sit at room temperature until supple enough to roll but still quite firm. It will continue to soften as you work. Roll the dough between 2 pieces of wax paper or between heavy plastic sheets from a plastic bag to a thickness of 1/8 inch. Turn the dough over once or twice while you are rolling it out to check for deep wrinkles; if necessary, peel off and smooth the paper or plastic over the dough before continuing to roll it. When the dough is thin enough, peel off the top sheet of paper or plastic and keep it in front of you. Invert the dough onto the sheet and peel off the second sheet. Cut as many large leaves as possible. Dip the edge of cookie cutters in flour as necessary to prevent sticking. Use the point of a paring knife to lift and remove scraps as you transfer cookies to cookie sheets. Place large cookies at least 1 1/2 inches apart on the cookie sheets. Cut a smaller leaf from the center of half of the large leaves. If the dough gets too soft at any time—while rolling, cutting, removing scraps between cookies, or transferring cookies—slide a cookie sheet underneath the paper or plastic and refrigerate the dough for a few minutes until firm. Repeat with the second piece of dough. Press all of the dough scraps together gently (don't overwork them with too much kneading), and reroll.

Bake 13 to 15 minutes, or until just beginning to color at the edges, rotating the cookie sheets from top to bottom and front to back halfway through the baking time to ensure even baking. (The small leaves may be baked 8 to 10 minutes on a separate cookie sheet to make miniature cookies, or the dough may be combined with other dough scraps to be rerolled and cut.)

Let cookies firm up on the pan for 1 to 2 minutes before transferring them to a rack with a metal pancake turner. Cool cookies completely before stacking or storing. Cookies are delicious fresh but even better the next day. *May be stored, airtight, for a month or more.*

To serve, spread each large solid leaf with a thin layer of preserves. Sieve powdered sugar over the empty leaves. Place a sugared empty leaf on top of each preserve-covered leaf.

### Variation

**Linzer Thumbprint Cookies:**
Form 1¹/₄-inch balls of
dough and place them 1¹/₂
inches apart on the cookie
sheets. Press the back of a
wooden spoon deeply into
each ball to form a depression (press the dough back
together if it cracks). Bake
the cookies for 14 to 16
minutes. Before serving,
spoon preserves or Lemon
Curd (page 20) into each
depression.

Tender nut-studded round or crescent-shape cookies rolled
powdered sugar turn up around the globe; only the nuts and the nam
are different. Use pecans to make Mexican Wedding Cakes, almon
for Viennese crescents or Greek kourabiedes, and walnuts for Russi
tea cakes. I like toasted and skinned hazelnuts (see page 111) as we
Try macadamias, Brazil nuts, hickory nuts, pistachios, or peanut

# Mexican Wedding Cakes

kes about 48 1 1/2-inch cookies

gredients

2 cups nuts
cup granulated sugar
cups all-purpose flour
teaspoon salt
tablespoons unsalted butter,
softened and cut into small
chunks
teaspoons vanilla extract
large egg yolk (optional)
cup powdered sugar

quipment

od processor
cookie sheets, ungreased

Pulse the nuts in the bowl of a food processor fitted with a steel blade until half of them look finely chopped and the rest look pulverized. Transfer the nuts to a bowl and set aside.

Wipe the bowl of the food processor with a paper towel to remove excess oil from the nuts. Put the granulated sugar in the processor and process until it is fine and powdery. Add the flour and salt and pulse just to mix. Add the butter, cut into small chunks, the vanilla, and the egg yolk if using. Process until the mixture looks damp and begins to clump together. Add the nuts and pulse just until combined. Transfer the dough to a bowl. Cover and refrigerate the dough for at least 2 hours, preferably overnight.

Preheat the oven to 325°F. Position the racks in the upper and lower thirds of the oven.

Shape slightly more than level tablespoons of dough into 1 1/4-inch balls or crescent shapes. Place 2 inches apart on cookie sheets. Bake for 22 to 24 minutes, or until lightly colored on top and golden brown on the bottom. Rotate the cookie sheets from top to bottom and front to back halfway through the baking time to ensure even baking.

While baking, put the powdered sugar in a small bowl. When the cookies are done, let them cool on the pan for 5 minutes, then sieve powdered sugar over the top of each one. Cool completely on a rack before storing. *May be stored, airtight, for at least 2 weeks.* Sieve additional powdered sugar over the cookies before serving if necessary.

(continued)

*These special butter cookies are characterized by a very delicate crumbly texture and rich flavor. The cookies hold their fat round or crescent shapes in the oven without spreading because the dough contains very little sugar and is mixed only enough to blend the ingredients together. The addition of an egg yolk makes an even richer flavor and more finely textured cookie.*

## Variation

**Nutty Thumbprint Cookies:** Mexican Wedding Cake dough is perfect—and f. more interesting than the usual—for thumbprint cookies. The dough holds it round shape and thumbprint depression in the oven; with so little sugar, it is perfect container for the sweet preserves traditional to this American classic The opportunity to pair the flavor of the filling with nuts in the cookie is also compelling. Apricot preserves are delicious with almond or hazelnut cookies, strawberry jam with peanuts, and so on. Chocolate is a happy partner for any of these nuts.

Prepare and chill Mexican Wedding Cake dough. Form 1¼-inch balls an place them on the cookie sheets. Press the back of a wooden spoon deeply into each ball to form a depression (press the dough back together if it crack. Bake and cool the cookies but do not roll them in powdered sugar. Before serving, spoon or pipe jam, jelly, or preserves into each depression. You will need about ½ cup of filling for 48 cookies.

**Other Ideas for Thumbprint Cookies:** Substitute dough for Linzer Cookies (page 37) or Peanut Butter Cookies (page 72). Fill cookies with your favorite frosting piped from a pastry bag or fill with Chocolate Ganache (page 21) or Lemon Curd (page 20).

Classic snicker doodles taste like delicate, crunchy rounds of cinnamon-topped French toast. Sometimes I add a cup of raisins.

# nicker Doodles

eheat the oven to 400°F. Position the racks in the upper and lower rds of the oven.

mbine the flour, cream of tartar, baking soda, and salt together in a wl and mix thoroughly with a whisk or fork. Set aside.

ith a large spoon in a medium mixing bowl or with a mixer, beat the tter with 1 1/2 cups of the sugar and the eggs just until smooth and ell blended but not fluffy. Add the dry ingredients and stir just until corporated. Gather the dough into a patty and wrap in plastic wrap. efrigerate until firm, at least 30 minutes.

lix the remaining 2 tablespoons of sugar and cinnamon in a small bowl. orm the dough into 1-inch balls. Roll the balls in cinnamon sugar and ace 2 inches apart on cookie sheets. Bake for 10 to 12 minutes, or until ghtly browned at the edges. Rotate cookie sheets from top to bottom nd front to back halfway through the baking time to ensure even baking.

se a metal pancake turner to transfer the cookies from the pan to ooling racks or slide the foil onto the racks. Cool the cookies completely efore stacking or storing. *May be stored, airtight, for several days.*

*Makes about 60 2 1/2-inch cookies*

### Ingredients

2 2/3 cups all-purpose flour
2 teaspoons cream of tartar
1 teaspoon baking soda
1/2 teaspoon salt
16 tablespoons unsalted butter, softened
1 1/2 cups plus 2 tablespoons sugar
2 large eggs
2 teaspoons ground cinnamon

### Equipment

2 cookie sheets, ungreased or lined with foil

chocolate-hazelnut meringue
kisses
46

faux florentines
47

chocolate chip cookies
48

double chocolate chip cookies
50

chocolate decadence cookies
52

robert's chocolate cookies
55

macadamia and white chocolate
chunk cookies
56

beacon hill cookies
57

chocolate wafers
58

ally, the chapter for people who don't think it's a cookie unless it has chocolate in it, on it, or between

America's love affair with the chocolate chip cookie is easily explained. What's not to like about a

nely sweet, soft but crunchy, caramelized cookie that delivers multiple bursts of barely melted choco-

e pleasure? From the irresistible accent of chocolate chips and chunks, to a tidal wave of chocolate in

ocolate Decadence Cookies, chocolate and cocoa offer us a myriad of taste and texture experiences.

chapter begins gently, with modest amounts of chocolate, and builds to a kind of bittersweet climax

h Chocolate Decadence Cookies and Robert's Chocolate Cookies. Don't miss my favorite Beacon Hill

okies, though, with their deceptively light texture but exceedingly rich chocolate flavor.

# Chocolate Cookies

*Here's what I learned:*

...For superior flavor, bake chocolate- and cocoa-based cookies on parchment paper to prevent the edges from scorching before the centers are baked.

...Better chocolate makes better cookies. Taste and experiment with the ever larger variety of quality domestic and imported chocolates available to the home cook.

...Save chocolate chips for use as chocolate chips. Use bar chocolate for melting or mixing into batters.

# Chocolate-Hazelnut Meringue Kisses

Preheat the oven to 200°F. Position racks in the upper and lower thirds of the oven.

Beat the egg whites with the cream of tartar and vanilla with a mixer at high speed until soft peaks form when the beaters are lifted. Add the sugar gradually, about 1 tablespoon at a time, continuing to beat until the egg whites are stiff and glossy. Use a large rubber spatula to fold the chocolate chips and nuts into the egg whites.

Drop slightly rounded teaspoons of batter 1 1/2 inches apart on the cookie sheets. Bake for about 2 hours, reversing the cookie sheets from top to bottom and front to back after 1 hour. Turn the oven off and let the cookies cool in the oven. Remove the cookies from the oven and set the pans on racks to cool completely before storing the cookies. *May be stored, airtight, for several weeks.*

## Variations

Low-Fat Meringue Kisses: Use only 1/4 cup each chocolate chips and nuts.

Mocha-Nut Meringue Kisses: Combine 2 teaspoons instant espresso powder with the sugar before adding it.

*Makes about 60 cookies*

**Ingredients**

3 large egg whites, at room temperature

1/8 teaspoon cream of tartar

1/2 teaspoon vanilla extract

2/3 cup sugar, preferably superfine

1/2 cup semisweet chocolate chips

1/2 cup hazelnuts, toasted and skinned, coarsely chopped (page 111)

**Equipment**

2 cookie sheets, lined with parchment paper

...miniscent of classic buttery caramelized
...rentines, these crisp oatmeal lace
...okies are far simpler to make and less
...tening—a double gift. I like them
...de with ginger as well as orange.

# ...aux Florentines

...heat the oven to 350°F. Position the racks in the upper and lower thirds of
...oven.

...t the eggs with the granulated sugar, brown sugar, vanilla and almond
...racts, orange zest, and salt with a mixer at high speed until very thick and
...t, about 3 minutes. Beat in the melted butter, then the baking powder,
...t until mixed. Stir in the oatmeal, candied peel, and chocolate chips.

...op level teaspoons of batter about 2 inches apart on cookie sheets. Bake
...10 to 12 minutes, or until the cookies are deep brown all over. Rotate the
...okie sheets top to bottom and front to back halfway through the baking time
...ensure even baking and watch carefully to avoid burning. Slide pan liners
...to cooling racks. Cool cookies completely before stacking or storing; they
...el from the liners easily when cool. Store airtight (up to 1 week) until serving
...retain crispness.

*Makes 45 to 50 cookies*

## Ingredients

3 large eggs
$3/4$ cup granulated sugar
$3/4$ cup (packed) light brown
   sugar, lump free
$3/4$ teaspoon vanilla extract
$1/8$ teaspoon almond extract
Finely grated zest of 1 orange
$1/2$ teaspoon salt
2 tablespoons unsalted butter,
   melted
4 teaspoons baking powder,
   sifted if lumpy
$3 1/2$ cups old-fashioned oatmeal
   (not quick or instant)
$3/4$ cup diced candied orange
   peel or 6 tablespoons minced
   crystallized ginger
1 cup semisweet chocolate chips

## Equipment

2 cookie sheets, lined with foil

A true American classic, buttery and irresistible, with cri
caramelized edges and rich chewy centers, lots of chocolate a
fresh, crunchy nuts. What makes these chocolate chip cookies
good? Melted butter, well chilled dough, cookie sheets witho
paper liners, and just the right temperatu

# Chocolate Chip Cookies

Combine the flour and baking soda in a bowl and mix together thoroughly with a whisk or a fork. Set aside.

Cut the butter into chunks and melt it in a large saucepan over medium heat. Remove the pan from the heat and stir in the granulated sugar, brown sugar, and salt. Mix in the eggs and vanilla. Stir in the flour mixture just until all of the dry ingredients are moistened. Let the mixture and the pan cool. Stir in the chocolate chips and the nuts. Cover and refrigerate for at least 2 hours, preferably overnight.

Preheat the oven to 375°F. Position the racks in the upper and lower thirds of the oven. Remove the dough from the refrigerator to soften. Scoop rounded tablespoons of dough and place them 3 inches apart on cookie sheets. Bake for 9 to 11 minutes, or until the cookies are golden brown at the edges and no longer look wet on top. Rotate baking sheets from top to bottom and front to back about halfway through the baking time to ensure even baking. Remove from the oven and let cookies firm up on the pan for 1 to 2 minutes. Use a metal pancake turner to transfer them to a rack to cool completely before storing or stacking. *May be stored in a tightly sealed container for several days.*

*Makes about 5 dozen cookies*

**Ingredients**

2 1/4 cups all-purpose flour
1 teaspoon baking soda
16 tablespoons unsalted butter
3/4 cup granulated sugar
3/4 cup (packed) brown sugar,
   lump free
1 teaspoon salt
2 large eggs
1 teaspoon vanilla extract
2 cups chocolate chips
1 cup coarsely chopped walnut
   or pecans

**Equipment**

2 cookie sheets, ungreased

### Variation

**Nut Clusters:** These are rich. Consider making them half size.

Omit the chocolate chips. Substitute 4 to 5 cups of any nut pieces you like for the walnuts. Macadamias are luxurious; toasted and skinned hazelnuts (see page 111) are sophisticated; salted peanuts or cashews are irresistible; Brazil nuts are unusual.

These cookies can be totally crunchy or crunchy on the edg
and soft within, depending on how long they are bake
Have fun substituting different nuts and/or adding good thin
like dried cherries, apricots, cranberries, or dic
crystallized ginger, or leave out the additions altogeth

# Double Chocolate Chip Cookies

Preheat the oven to 350°F. if you plan to bake cookies immediately after mixing, otherwise wait until you are ready to bake. Position the racks in the upper and lower thirds of the oven.

Combine the flour, cocoa, baking soda, baking powder, and salt in a medium bowl and mix together thoroughly with a whisk or a fork. Set aside.

Beat the butter, granulated sugar, and brown sugar with the back of a spoon in a large mixing bowl or with a mixer until smooth and creamy but not very fluffy, less than 1 1/2 minutes with an electric mixer. Mix in the egg and vanilla. Add the flour mixture and mix just until incorporated. Stir in the nuts and chocolate chips.

To bake the cookies immediately: Scoop slightly rounded tablespoons of dough and place about 2 inches apart on cookie sheet.

To bake the cookies later: Form the dough into an 11 X 1 3/4-inch log. Wrap it in foil and refrigerate for at least 2 hours, but preferably 12 hours or up to 3 days. *(Dough may also be frozen for up to 3 months.)* Use a sharp knife to cut the log into slices 3/8 inch thick. Place the slices at least 1 1/2 inches apart on cookie sheets.

*Makes about 30 2 1/2 - inch cookies*

### Ingredients

1 cup all-purpose flour
1/2 cup unsweetened cocoa powder, preferably Dutch process
1/2 teaspoon baking soda
1/4 teaspoon baking powder
1/8 teaspoon salt
8 tablespoons unsalted butter, softened
1/2 cup granulated sugar
1/2 cup (packed) brown sugar, lump free
1 large egg
1 teaspoon vanilla extract
1/2 cup chopped walnuts
1/2 cup chocolate chips

e fresh scoops or cold slices for 12 to 14 minutes. Cookies will puff up
then settle down slightly when they are done. Rotate baking sheets
m top to bottom and front to back about halfway through the baking time
ensure even baking. Use a pancake turner to transfer cookies from the
to a cooling rack, or slide the sheet of parchment onto the rack. Cool
mpletely before storing or stacking. *May be stored in a tightly sealed
ntainer for up to 2 weeks.*

**riations**

**uble Chocolate Mint Cookies:** Add 3/8 teaspoon peppermint extract with
sugar. Omit the walnuts and increase the chocolate chips to 1 cup, either
misweet or white chocolate.

**uble Chocolate Mocha Cookies:** Dissolve 2 1/2 teaspoons instant espresso
wder in the vanilla or add 3 tablespoons fresh coarsely ground espresso
other dark roasted) coffee beans.

**icy Chocolate-Pecan Cookies:** Add 1/2 teaspoon ground cinnamon, a gener-
s pinch of ground cayenne, and a generous pinch of ground black pepper
th the sugar. Substitute 1 cup of pecan pieces for the walnuts and omit
e chocolate chips.

**Equipment**

2 cookie sheets, lined
   with parchment paper
   or ungreased

*The basic cookie is
good on its own:
chocolatey without
being intensely rich or
overly sweet. Though
this dough is similar to
conventional chocolate
chip cookie dough, the
ideal baking temperature
is 350°F. rather than
375°F. and melting the
butter does not improve
the cookies. The cookies
are at their very best
if the batter is chilled
before baking.*

Narsai David, friend, radio host, and former chef and restaurateur, responsible for making several memorable chocolate desse famous. Nearly flourless, this one is the ne plus ultra of chocola cookies and a close cousin of Narsai's Mudslic

# Chocolate Decadence Cookies

Preheat the oven to 350°F. if you plan to bake the cookies immediately after mixing, otherwise wait until you are ready to bake. Position racks in the upper and lower thirds of the oven.

Whisk the eggs with the sugar and vanilla in a small bowl to combine thoroughly. Set the bowl in a larger bowl of hot tap water while preparing the rest of the ingredients.

Combine the flour, baking powder, and salt in another small bowl and mix thoroughly together with a whisk or fork.

Put the chopped chocolate (not the chips) and the butter in a large heatproof bowl in a skillet of barely simmering water. Stir frequently until melted and smooth. Or microwave on medium power for 2 to 2 1/2 minutes, stirring once or twice, or until the chocolate is melted. Remove from the heat. Chocolate should be warm, not hot. Add the egg mixture to the chocolate, stirring just until thoroughly combined. Stir in the flour mixture, then the nuts and chocolate chips.

To bake the cookies immediately: Scoop slightly rounded tablespoons of batter and place them 1 1/2 inches apart on the cookie sheets. Bake for 10 to 12 minutes, or until the surface of the cookie looks dry and set and the centers are still gooey.

*Makes 30 2 1/2 - inch cookies*

### Ingredients

2 large eggs
1/2 cup sugar
1 teaspoon vanilla extract
1/4 cup all-purpose flour
1/4 teaspoon baking powder
1/8 teaspoon salt
8 ounces bittersweet or
  semisweet chocolate, coarse
  chopped
2 tablespoons unsalted butter
2 cups walnuts or pecans,
  coarsely chopped or left in
  large pieces
6 ounces semisweet
  chocolate chips

### Equipment

2 cookie sheets, lined with
  parchment paper or greased

bake the cookies later: Tear off 2 sheets of aluminum foil about 16 inches
g. Scrape half of the dough down the center of 1 sheet of foil, forming a
p of dough about 10 inches long. Bring up the sides of the sheet to shape
 dough into an 11 X 1½-inch log. Repeat with the second sheet. If the
ter is too soft to hold a log shape, let it rest for a couple of minutes to
n up. Refrigerate the logs until firm, 30 to 60 minutes or up to 2 days.
e dough may be frozen for up to 2 months.)

nen ready to bake, preheat the oven and position the racks as described
ove. Cut each log into slices ¾ inch thick and place them 1½ inches
art on the cookie sheets. Bake for 12 to 14 minutes, or until the surfaces
 dry and cracked and the centers are still gooey. Rotate the sheets from
ck to front and top to bottom halfway through the baking time to ensure
en baking.

de the parchment sheet onto cooling racks or use a metal pancake turner
transfer cookies from the pan to the racks. Cool completely before storing
stacking. *May be stored in a tightly sealed container for 2 to 3 days.*

*Just imagine an intensely
bittersweet chocolate
brownie with nuts and
chocolate chips and a
crunchy exterior. If the
batter is scooped and
baked immediately after
mixing, the cookies are
voluptuously lumpy with
a thin crust and a soft,
luscious center conceal-
ing nuts and chocolate
pieces. If the batter is
chilled and sliced before
baking, the cookies
develop appealing earth-
quake cracks, with nuts
and chocolate pieces
revealed and a more
dramatic contrast of
crunchy exterior with
soft center. Have it
your way.*

I love these cookies. Robert Steinberg created the recipe for his compa[ny] Scharffen Berger Chocolate Maker, the first and only micro chocola[te] manufacturer in the United States. The cookies are a defining statement abo[ut] chocolate for the sophisticated palate. They are only slightly swe[et] but rich and gooey, and laced with tiny chunks of the finest *unsweetene[d]* chocolate in the world. (If you cannot use Scharffen Berger Chocolat[e] follow the substitutions in the recipe, since most other unsweetene[d] chocolates are too harsh and gritty to enjoy as chunks[.]

# Robert's Chocolate Cookies

...kes 50 small or 25 large cookies

**...redients**

...) 10 ounces unsweetened
Scharffen Berger Chocolate
...or 6 ounces of any other
unsweetened baking chocolate
and 3 to 4 ounces of premium-
quality bittersweet chocolate)
. cup all-purpose flour
. teaspoon baking powder
. teaspoon salt
...ablespoons unsalted butter
...arge eggs, at room
temperature
.../3 cups sugar
.../2 teaspoons finely ground,
freshly ground coffee
...teaspoon vanilla extract
. cup walnut pieces (optional)

**...quipment**

... cookie sheets, lined with
parchment paper

Divide the Scharffen Berger chocolate into two portions as follows: Chop 6 ounces for melting and cut 3 to 4 ounces into chunks about the size of large chocolate chips. If using a brand other than Scharffen Berger, use the unsweetened for melting and the bittersweet for chunks. Set aside.

Combine the flour, baking powder, and salt in a small bowl and mix together thoroughly with a whisk or fork. Set aside. Melt the butter with the 6 ounces of chocolate in a double boiler over barely simmering water, stirring occasionally, until melted and smooth. Remove from the heat and set aside.

Beat the eggs with the sugar, coffee, and vanilla with a mixer until pale and thick, about 5 minutes. Stir in the chocolate mixture with a rubber spatula. Stir in the flour mixture followed by the chocolate chunks and the nuts, if using them. Cover and refrigerate until firm, about an hour, or up to 4 days.

Preheat the oven to 350°F. Position the racks in the upper and lower thirds of the oven. Drop level tablespoons of batter for small cookies or heaping table-spoons (equivalent of 2 level tablespoons) for large cookies, 2 inches apart on the cookie sheets. Bake until cookies are puffed, dry, and crackled on the surface but soft and gooey within, 8 to 10 minutes for small cookies, 10 to 12 minutes for large cookies. Rotate the cookie sheets from top to bottom and front to back halfway through baking time to ensure even baking. Slide the parchment paper onto racks to cool completely before storing or stacking. *May be kept, airtight, for 2 days at room temperature.*

# Macadamia and White Chocolate Chunk Cookies

Pulverize the oats in the processor or blender until fine. Add the flour, baking soda, and salt and pulse to combine. Set aside.

Cut the butter into chunks and melt in a large saucepan over medium heat. Remove from the heat and stir in the granulated sugar, brown sugar, and vanilla. Whisk in the egg. Stir in the flour mixture just until all of the dry ingredients are moistened. Let the mixture cool for a few minutes if it is at all warm. Stir in the nuts and chocolate chips. Cover and refrigerate overnight.

Preheat the oven to 325°F. Position the racks in the upper and lower thirds of the oven.

Remove the dough from the refrigerator to soften. Scoop rounded tablespoons of dough and place about 2 inches apart on the cookie sheets. Bake for 13 to 15 minutes, or until the cookies are deep golden brown. Rotate cookie sheets from top to bottom and front to back about halfway through the baking time to ensure even baking. Use a metal pancake turner to transfer cookies to racks to cool completely before storing or stacking. *May be stored, airtight, for several days.*

*Makes about 3 dozen cookies*

**Ingredients**

3/4 cup rolled oats
3/4 cup all-purpose flour
1/2 teaspoon baking soda
1/4 teaspoon salt
8 tablespoons unsalted butter
1/3 cup granulated sugar
1/3 cup (packed) brown sugar, lump free
1/2 teaspoon vanilla extract
1 large egg
1 cup coarsely chopped dry-roasted salted macadamia nuts
1 cup white chocolate chips

**Equipment**

Food processor or blender
2 cookie sheets, ungreased or lined with foil

ese satisfying morsels are light and delicately crisp
 the outside—but chocolatey rich and moist within.
friend gave me the recipe for these cookies, telling
e he loved them when he was a little boy. I reduced
e sugar by half and substituted a good-quality bitter-
weet chocolate for the original chocolate chips, and
w they taste exactly as he wants to remember them!

# eacon Hill Cookies

eheat the oven to 350°F. Position racks in the upper and lower thirds of
e oven.

elt the chocolate in a heatproof bowl in the microwave on medium power
2 to 2¹/₂ minutes, or set the bowl in a skillet of barely simmering water.
r frequently until the chocolate is almost completely melted. Remove from
e heat and stir to complete the melting. Set aside.

eat the egg whites with the cream of tartar and vanilla until soft peaks
rm when you lift the beaters. Add the sugar gradually, continuing to beat
til the egg whites are stiff but not dry. Pour the nuts and all of the warm
ocolate over the egg whites. Fold with a rubber spatula until the color is
iform. Do not let the batter wait.

op level teaspoons of batter at least 1 inch apart on the cookie sheets.
ake for 10 to 12 minutes, or until the cookies are shiny and cracked, firm
hen you press them but still gooey inside. Rotate the sheets from front to
ack and top to bottom of the oven about halfway through the baking time
ensure even baking. Slide the parchment liners onto racks or transfer
dividual cookies from the pan with a metal pancake turner. Cool cookies
mpletely. Cookies are best on the day they are baked but still delectable
couple of days later. *May be stored, airtight, for 2 to 3 days.*

*Makes about 30 2-inch cookies*

## Ingredients

6 ounces bittersweet or
   semisweet chocolate,
   cut into pieces
2 large egg whites, at room
   temperature
¹/₈ teaspoon cream of tartar
¹/₂ teaspoon vanilla extract
¹/₄ cup sugar
³/₄ cup chopped walnuts

## Equipment

2 cookie sheets, lined with
   parchment paper or greased

These cookies are reduced fat, but don't pass the
by for that reason. They are tender, crisp, and flavor
and far better than commercial chocolate wafers. You m
use either Dutch process or natural cocoa. The bett
quality the cocoa, however, the better the cookie

# Chocolate Wafers

Combine the flour, cocoa, baking soda, and salt in a small bowl and mix
together thoroughly with a whisk or fork. Set aside.

Beat the butter and margarine with an electric mixer for a few seconds just
until blended. Add the granulated sugar, brown sugar, and vanilla and beat
at high speed for about 1 minute.

Beat in the egg white. Add the flour mixture and mix on low speed, just until
incorporated. Gather the dough together with your hands and form it into
a 9- to 10-inch log. Wrap the log in wax paper or foil. Fold or twist the ends
of the paper without pinching or flattening the log. Refrigerate for at least
45 minutes, or until needed.

Preheat the oven to 350°F. Position racks in the upper and lower thirds of
the oven.

Use a sharp knife to cut the dough log into slices a scant 1/4 inch thick. Place
1 inch apart on cookie sheets. Bake for 12 to 14 minutes, or until the cookies
puff and crackle on top, then begin to settle down slightly. Rotate baking
sheets from top to bottom and front to back about halfway through the

*Makes 40 to 45 cookies*

**Ingredients**

1 cup all-purpose flour
1/2 cup plus 1 tablespoon
    unsweetened cocoa powder,
    preferably Dutch process
1/4 teaspoon baking soda
1/4 teaspoon salt
3 tablespoons unsalted butter,
    slightly softened
3 tablespoons stick margarine
1/2 cup plus 1 tablespoon
    granulated sugar
1/2 cup plus 1 tablespoon
    (packed) brown sugar,
    lump free
1 teaspoon vanilla extract
1 large egg white

ing time to ensure even baking. Slide the parchment or foil onto cooling
s. Cool the cookies completely before storing or stacking. *May be*
*ed, airtight, for up to 2 weeks.*

**iations**

xican Chocolate Wafers: Add 1/2 teaspoon ground cinnamon, a generous
ch of cayenne, and a generous pinch of ground black pepper with the
ars.

ocolate Espresso Wafers: Add 1 1/2 tablespoons instant espresso powder
h the sugars.

nt Chocolate Wafers: Add 1/4 teaspoon peppermint extract to the butter
d sugars.

**Equipment**

2 cookie sheets, lined with
parchment paper or foil

*For crisp edges and
chewy instead of crisp
centers, bake Chocolate
Wafers a little less time
and serve on the same
day they are baked.*

coconut macaroons
62

lemon ginger wafers
66

peanut butter
cookies
72

bridget's oat-
coconut coo
76

almond macaroons
64

maya's lemon wafers
69

cashew cookies
74

moravian spice c
77

coconut sticks
65

rugelach
70

oatmeal cookies
75

ginger snap
79

okies connect many of us to childhood pleasures. Images and memories come instantly, unbidden, en with a single bite. I baked and tasted countless versions of old-fashioned cookies, often with a dhood memory attached, in order to select recipes for this collection. The memories were still delicious, the cookies themselves needed a little tweaking. So, I added ginger and spice to Ginger Snaps, and led around endlessly to make Oatmeal Cookies with crisp caramelized edges, chewy centers, and flavor of toasted oats. I simplified, amplified, and adjusted. The end result? Simple but delicious okies. Make 'em big to go with a tall glass of milk or mini to accompany a demitasse. Most are as mfortable in the lunch box as they are on a silver tray. When a cookie is good, plain *is* fancy.

# Cookie Classics

**Here's what I learned**

...Any hand-shaped or rolled-and-cut cookie can also be made quickly and efficiently by shaping the dough into a log, then chilling and slicing to the desired thickness. For very thin cookies this takes a thin sharp knife and good control, but it is always faster and less fussy than rolling and cutting.

...Fresh spices and hand-grated nutmeg are the key to big bright flavors in any cookie that contains spices.

...To fine-tune the baking of a given batch of cookies, test bake four cookies, and remove two of them a minute or two earlier than the others. Note both the baking time and appearance of the cookies, since it may take a little longer to bake the cookies when the oven is filled. Cool the cookies before tasting them to decide just how you like them. This is a good way to see how the same cookies vary in flavor, crunch, and chewiness, depending on how long they are baked.

Crisp and chewy with dark golden brown shreds
coconut on the outside. Insides are soft and moist, swe
and coconutty. When half-dipped in melted bitterswe
chocolate (see page 17), these cookies are reminiscent of
and even better than—a certain popular candy ba

# Coconut Macaroons

Preheat the oven to 350°F. Position racks in the upper and lower thirds of
the oven.

Combine all of the ingredients in a large heatproof mixing bowl, preferably
stainless steel, because the ingredients heat up faster than in glass. Set the
bowl in a skillet of barely simmering water and stir the mixture, scraping
the bottom to prevent burning, until it is very hot to the touch and the egg
whites have thickened, about 6 to 7 minutes. It is ready when a scoop of
batter on the cookie sheet holds a soft shape without a puddle of syrup
forming around it.

Scoop 2 tablespoons of the mixture about 2 inches apart on the cookie
sheets. Bake for 13 to 15 minutes, or until the edges of the cookies and the
protruding coconut shreds are deep golden brown. Rotate the sheets from
front to back and upper to lower about halfway through the baking time to
ensure even baking. Slide the parchment onto a rack. Cool the cookies
completely before removing them from the paper. The cookies are most
delicious on the day they are baked—the exterior is crisp and chewy and
the interior soft and moist. *The cookies will soften. May be stored, airtight,
for 4 to 5 days.*

*Makes 22 2 1/4- inch cookies*

**Ingredients**

4 large egg whites
3 cups sweetened shredded
    coconut (9 ounces)
3/4 cup sugar
2 teaspoons vanilla extract
Scant 1/4 teaspoon salt

**Equipment**

2 cookie sheets, lined with
    parchment paper

# Almond Macaroons

In a food processor fitted with a steel blade, combine the almonds and sugar. Process until the almonds are very fine and the mixture is beginning to pack together around the sides of the bowl, at least 3 minutes. Add the almond extract. With the processor on, gradually add only enough of the egg white to form a ball of dough around the blade. With the processor still running, add only enough additional egg white so that the dough has the consistency of very thick, sticky mashed potatoes and no longer forms a ball. Drop rounded teaspoons (equivalent to 2 level teaspoons) 2 inches apart on the cookie sheets. Smooth the top of each cookie with a moistened pastry brush or your fingertips. Let the cookies stand for 30 minutes before baking them.

Preheat the oven to 300°F. Position the racks in the upper and lower thirds of the oven. Bake the cookies for 20 to 25 minutes, or until the edges of the cookies barely begin to color. Rotate the pans from front to back and top to bottom about halfway through the baking time to ensure even baking. Slide the parchment onto racks. Cool the cookies completely before detaching them from the parchment. *May be stored, airtight, for 2 to 3 days at room temperature.*

*Makes 55 2-inch cookies*

### Ingredients

7 ounces blanched almonds
(1 1/3 cups whole or
1 2/3 cups slivered)
1 1/2 cups sugar
1 1/2 teaspoons almond extract
3 to 4 large egg whites

### Equipment

2 cookie sheets, lined with
parchment paper

# ：oconut Sticks

㎎ the back of a large spoon or with an electric mixer, in a medium bowl
the butter with the sugar and salt until smooth and creamy, not at all
y. Mix in the vanilla. Mix in the coconut. Add the flour and mix with your
ers, pinching and gathering the mixture until it resembles damp crumbs.
zle in the water and continue to mix with your fingers, pinching and
ering the dough until the water seems well distributed. The dough will
form a smooth, cohesive mass; it will be crumbly, but it will stick together
n you press it. Turn it out on a large sheet of foil. Press the dough into a
9-inch rectangle a scant 1/2 inch thick. Fold the foil over the rectangle, and
p the dough airtight. Slide a cookie sheet under the package and refrigerate
r 2 hours or overnight.

heat the oven to 350°F. Position racks in the upper and lower thirds of
oven.

a long sharp knife to trim 1 short edge of the dough rectangle. Then cut
ice a scant 3/8 inch wide. Use the knife to transfer the slice to the cookie
et, placing it cut side up. Cut and transfer each slice, placing them at least
ch apart. If some break, just push them back together or bake them broken;
y will look and taste great anyway.

ke for 12 to 14 minutes, or until the cookies just begin to turn golden at the
es. Rotate the cookie sheets from top to bottom and front to back halfway
ough the baking time to ensure even baking.

de the parchment carefully onto a rack or set the pan itself on a rack to cool.
ol cookies completely before stacking or storing. Cookies are most delicious
the day they are baked. *May be stored, airtight, for several days.*

*Makes about 32 6-inch sticks*

## Ingredients

6 tablespoons unsalted butter,
   softened
2/3 cup sugar
1/4 teaspoon salt
1 teaspoon vanilla extract
1 cup unsweetened dried coconut
   (available at health food stores,
   or by mail order)
1 cup plus 2 tablespoons
   all-purpose flour
2 tablespoons water

## Equipment

1 or 2 cookie sheets, lined with
   parchment paper or greased

# Lemon Ginger Wafers

Combine the flour, baking soda, and ground ginger in a medium bowl and mix together thoroughly with a whisk or a fork. Set aside.

Using a spoon, mix the egg, the egg yolk, and sugar in a large bowl until homogeneous. Mix in the melted butter, fresh ginger, lemon zest, and salt. Add the dry ingredients and stir just until incorporated. Cover and chill at least 20 minutes. Divide the dough into fourths. Roll each piece 1/16 inch thick between 2 sheets of plastic from a plastic bag or wax paper. Slide a cookie sheet under the plastic or wax paper and dough. Refrigerate until firm, about 15 minutes or up to 2 days.

Preheat the oven to 400°F. Position racks in the upper and lower thirds of the oven.

Remove 1 piece of dough from the refrigerator. Peel the top sheet of plastic or paper from the dough, reserving the sheet. Invert the dough onto it and peel off the second sheet. Use a cookie cutter to cut out 2 1/2-inch cookies or any desired size or shape. Place cookies 1 inch apart on cookie sheets. Repeat with remaining dough. Scraps may be pressed together and rerolled. Bake for 6 to 7 minutes, or until lightly browned at the edges. Rotate the sheets from top to bottom and front to back halfway through the baking time to ensure even baking. Slide the parchment liners onto racks or use a metal pancake turner to transfer cookies from the pan to a rack. Cool cookies completely before stacking or storing. Store cookies in an airtight container as soon as they are cool. *May be stored, airtight, for at least 1 week.*

*Makes 64 2 1/2 - inch cookies*

**Ingredients**

2 1/4 cups all-purpose flour
1/4 teaspoon baking soda
1 teaspoon ground ginger
1 large egg
1 large egg yolk
1 cup sugar
12 tablespoons unsalted butter, melted and cooled
2 tablespoons grated fresh ginger
1 tablespoon finely grated lemon zest
1/4 teaspoon salt

**Equipment**

2 cookie sheets, lined with parchment paper or greased
2 1/2-inch cookie cutters, round or any shape

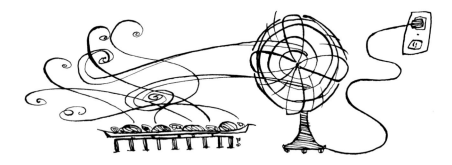

*Cool cookies completely before stacking*
*or storing. Store cookies in an airtight container*
*as soon as they are cool.*

My friend and assistant, Maya Klein, invented these tender, crisp, and very lemony wafers. A plain but superb cookie to serve with tea or to accompany fresh fruit sorbets for dessert.

# aya's Lemon Wafers

at the lemon juice in a small nonreactive saucepan over high heat. Boil for
out 5 minutes, or until thick and syrupy and reduced to about 1 tablespoon.
d the butter and stir until melted. Set aside.

mbine the flour and baking soda in a medium bowl and mix together
roughly with a whisk or a fork. Set aside.

ng a spoon or a rubber spatula, mix the egg, egg yolk, and sugar in a large
wl until homogeneous. Mix in the butter mixture, lemon zest, and salt.
d the dry ingredients and stir just until incorporated. Cover and chill at least
minutes. Divide the dough into 4 pieces. Roll each piece 1/16 inch thick
tween 2 sheets of plastic from a plastic bag or wax paper. Slide a cookie
eet under the plastic sheets and dough. Refrigerate until firm, about 15
nutes or up to 2 days.

eheat the oven to 400°F. Position racks in the upper and lower thirds of
e oven.

move 1 piece of dough from the refrigerator. Peel off and reserve the top
eet of plastic or paper. Invert the dough onto it and peel off the second
eet. Use a cookie cutter to cut out 2 1/2-inch cookies or any desired size
shape. Place cookies 1 inch apart on the cookie sheets. Repeat with the
maining dough. Scraps may be pressed together and rerolled. Bake for 6 to
minutes, or until lightly browned at the edges. Rotate the sheets from top
bottom and front to back halfway through the baking time to ensure even
aking. Slide the parchment liners onto racks or use a metal pancake turner
transfer cookies from the pan to a rack. Cool cookies completely before
acking or storing. Store cookies in an airtight container as soon as they are
ol. *May be stored for at least 1 week.*

## ariation

emon Poppy Seed Wafers: Add 1/4 cup poppy seeds with the flour mixture.

*Makes 64 2 1/2-inch cookies*

## Ingredients

1/4 cup fresh lemon juice
12 tablespoons unsalted butter,
  cut into several pieces
2 1/4 cups all-purpose flour
1/4 teaspoon baking soda
1 large egg
1 large egg yolk
1 cup sugar
4 teaspoons finely grated
  lemon zest
1/4 teaspoon salt

## Equipment

2 cookie sheets, lined with
  parchment paper or greased
2 1/2-inch cookie cutter, round or
  any shape

Rugelach are more like miniature flaky pastries th
cookies, but they are simple and fun to make. Dream
your own filling ideas if you like, although the class
sugar, cinnamon, nuts, and currants is hard to be

# Rugelach

To make the dough: Combine the flour, sugar, and salt in the bowl of a food processor fitted with a steel blade. Pulse a few times to mix. Cut the butter into 8 pieces and add to the flour mixture. Pulse until the butter pieces are about the size of breadcrumbs. Cut the cream cheese into 4 pieces and add to the mixture. Process until the dough begins to clump together, about 30 seconds. Divide the dough into 4 pieces. Press each piece into a flat patty about 4 inches in diameter. Wrap and refrigerate until firm, about 4 hours.

Preheat the oven to 350°F. Position racks in the upper and lower thirds of the oven.

To make the filling: Mix together the granulated sugar, brown sugar, cinnamon, walnuts, and currants in a medium bowl.

Remove 1 piece of dough from the refrigerator. Roll between 2 pieces of wax paper into a 12-inch circle a scant 1/8 inch thick. Peel the top sheet of wax paper from the dough and place it on the counter or a cutting board. Flip the dough over onto the paper and peel off the second sheet. Sprinkle a quarter of the filling over the dough. Roll over the filling with a rolling pin to press it gently into the dough.

*Makes 48 pieces*

**Ingredients**

Dough:
2 1/2 cups all-purpose flour
2 tablespoons granulated sugar
1/4 teaspoon salt
16 tablespoons unsalted butter, cold
8 ounces cream cheese, cold

Filling:
2 tablespoons granulated sugar
1/2 cup (packed) brown sugar, lump free
1 teaspoon ground cinnamon
1 cup finely chopped walnuts
1/2 cup dried currants

**Equipment**

Food processor
2 cookie sheets, lined with parchment paper or foil

the dough like a pie into 12 equal wedges. Roll the wide outside edge up
and the filling toward the point. Place the roll, with the dough point under-
th to prevent it from unrolling, on a cookie sheet. Repeat with the remaining
dges, placing cookies 1 1/2 inches apart. If at any time the dough becomes too
t to roll, return it to the refrigerator to firm up. Roll, cut, and fill the remaining
ces of dough. Bake about 25 minutes, or until light golden brown at the
ges. Rotate the sheets from top to bottom and front to back halfway through
baking time to ensure even baking. Set the baking sheets on racks to cool.
ol the rugelach completely before storing or stacking. Rugelach are best on
day they are baked. *May be stored, airtight, for about 5 days.*

### riations

**ricot-Nut Rugelach:** Process 1 cup apricot jam or preserves in a food proces-
if there are large pieces of fruit. Mix with 1/2 teaspoon ground cinnamon. Roll
t the Rugelach dough as described. Spread each piece with one quarter of the
n mixture, then sprinkle with 1/4 cup of finely chopped walnuts. Roll up and
ke as described.

**ocolate-Hazelnut Rugelach:** Combine 1/2 cup sugar, 1 teaspoon vanilla extract,
up finely chopped toasted and skinned hazelnuts (see page 111), and 1 cup
iniature chocolate chips. Use in place of filling, as directed.

**ate-Nut Rugelach:** Stuff 48 whole pitted dates each with a walnut or pecan
lf. Roll the Rugelach wedges around the stuffed dates.

My ideal peanut butter cookie is crunchy, very peanutty, and not t
sweet. Chilling the dough improves the flavor, but if you must m
and bake the cookies immediately, use melted instead of soften
butter to boost the flavor, and expect a slightly chewier cook

# Peanut Butter Cookies

Mix the flour and baking soda together thoroughly with a whisk or fork.
Set aside.

Using the back of a large spoon in a large bowl or with an electric mixer,
mix the butter, the brown and granulated sugars, and salt until smooth and
creamy, not fluffy. Add the egg, vanilla, and peanut butter and mix until
homogeneous. Add the flour mixture and stir just until incorporated. Wrap
and refrigerate the dough for at least 2 hours, if not 12 hours.

Preheat the oven to 325°F. Position racks in the upper and lower thirds of
the oven.

Scoop (slightly more than 1 level tablespoon) and form dough into 1 1/4-inch
balls. Place the balls 2 inches apart on cookie sheets. Flatten each ball to
a thickness of 3/8 inch with a fork, pressing the back of the tines into the
dough in two directions. Or, partially flatten the balls with the bottom of a
glass and then press each cookie with a cookie stamp or other textured
object. Bake for 14 to 16 minutes, or until colored on top and golden brown
underneath. Rotate the sheets from front to back and top to bottom about
halfway through the baking time to ensure even baking. Cool cookies completely before stacking or storing. *May be stored, airtight, for at least 2 weeks.*

*Makes about 3 dozen
2 1/4- inch cookies*

### Ingredients

1 1/3 cups all-purpose flour
1/2 teaspoon baking soda
8 tablespoons unsalted butter,
    softened
1/4 cup (packed) dark brown
    sugar, lump free, or 1/2 cup
    (packed) light brown sugar
3/4 cup granulated sugar with
    dark brown sugar or 1/2 cup
    with light brown sugar
1/2 teaspoon salt
1 large egg
1 teaspoon vanilla extract
1 1/4 cups natural chunky
    peanut butter

### Equipment

2 cookie sheets, lined with
    parchment paper

## Variations

### Design Ideas:
This dough holds an imprint well: for alternatives to the traditional fork crosshatch, try pressing the dough with cookie stamps, clean rubber stamps, meat mallets, graters, serrated knives, cake combs, or any household item with an intriguing surface.

### Mini Peanut Butter Cookies:
These are especially crunchy.
Form 2 level teaspoons into 1-inch balls before flattening. Bake for 14 to 16 minutes. Makes about 65 minis.

### Peanut Butter Thumbprints:
Form 2 level teaspoons into 1-inch balls, press the back of a wooden spoon into each, and bake for 14 to 16 minutes. Fill with jam or Chocolate Ganache (page 21). Makes about 65 thumbprints.

# Cashew Cookies

Measure and set aside 1 cup of the cashews. Place the remaining nuts in the bowl of a food processor fitted with a steel blade. Add the brown sugar, granulated sugar, and salt. Process for 3 minutes or more, scraping down the bowl and breaking up clumps 3 or 4 times, until the nuts are very finely ground and the mixture forms a stiff oily mass around the blade. Cut the butter into chunks and add it to the bowl. Add the egg and the vanilla. Process until the mixture forms a mass (it's OK if the oil from the nuts is not completely incorporated). Whisk the flour and baking soda together and add it to the mixture. Pulse until the flour is partially incorporated. Add the reserved cashews and pulse just until the flour is no longer visible and the nuts are coarsely chopped. Remove the dough from the processor and knead it with your hands a few times to finish the mixing. The dough will be very oily. Divide the dough in half and form two 8 X 2-inch logs. Wrap the logs in foil and refrigerate for at least 2 hours or overnight.

Preheat the oven to 350°F. Position racks in the upper and lower thirds of the oven.

Slice the chilled dough 1/4 to 3/8 inch thick and place slices at least 1 1/2 inches apart on the cookie sheets. Bake for 12 to 14 minutes, or until golden brown at the edges. Rotate the sheets from front to back and top to bottom of the oven about halfway through the baking period to ensure even baking. Slide the parchment sheets onto racks or transfer cookies from the pan with a metal pancake turner. Cool completely before stacking or storing. *May be stored, airtight, for at least 2 weeks.*

*Makes about 45 2 1/2 - inch cookie*

### Ingredients

1 pound whole raw unsalted cashews (available in health food or grocery stores that sell nuts in bulk)
1/2 cup (packed) light brown sugar, lump free
1/2 cup granulated sugar
1/2 teaspoon salt
8 tablespoons unsalted butter
1 large egg
1 teaspoon vanilla extract
1 1/3 cups all-purpose flour
1/2 teaspoon baking soda

### Equipment

Food processor
2 cookie sheets, lined with parchment paper or ungrease

elted butter is one key to the flavor and texture of
ese great cookies. Overnight chilling allows the
ts to absorb the dough's moisture. The cookies
e baked directly on the pan, not on parchment
per, and at a low temperature, to produce great
asted oat flavor, caramelized crunchy brown
ges, and flavorful chewy centers. Perfection!

# atmeal Cookies

ix the flour, rolled oats, baking soda, cinnamon, and nutmeg together
oroughly with a whisk or fork. Set aside.

ut the butter into chunks and melt in a large saucepan over medium heat.
emove from the heat and stir in the brown sugar, granulated sugar, vanilla,
d salt. Whisk in the eggs. Stir in the flour mixture just until all of the dry
gredients are moistened. Stir in the walnuts and raisins. Cover and
frigerate overnight.

eheat the oven to 325°F. Position racks in the upper and lower thirds of
e oven.

or large cookies, scoop about 2 level tablespoons of dough and place the
ookies about 3 inches apart on the cookie sheet. For small cookies, scoop
level tablespoon of dough. Bake for 15 to 17 minutes for large cookies,
3 to 15 minutes for small cookies, or until the cookies are deep golden
own. Rotate sheets from top to bottom and front to back about halfway
rough the baking time to ensure even baking. Use a metal pancake turner
transfer cookies to a rack to cool completely before storing or stacking.
*May be stored, airtight, for several days.*

*Makes 40 3 1/4- inch cookies or
80 2 1/2- inch cookies*

**Ingredients**

1 cup plus 2 tablespoons
    all-purpose flour
2 cups rolled oats
1 teaspoon baking soda
1 teaspoon ground cinnamon
1/4 teaspoon ground nutmeg
16 tablespoons unsalted butter
3/4 cup (packed) light brown
    sugar, lump free
3/4 cup granulated sugar
1 teaspoon vanilla extract
1/2 teaspoon salt
2 large eggs
1 cup chopped walnuts
1 cup raisins

**Equipment**

2 cookie sheets, greased

# Bridget's Oat-Raisin-Coconut Cookies

This treat was adapted from a splendid recipe from the Bovine Bakery in Point Reyes Station, California.

Combine the flour, rolled oats, baking soda, cinnamon, and nutmeg in a medium bowl and mix together thoroughly with a whisk or fork. Set aside.

Cut the butter into chunks and melt in a large saucepan over medium heat. Remove the pan from the heat and stir in the brown sugar, granulated sugar, vanilla, and salt. Whisk in the eggs. Stir in the flour mixture just until all of the dry ingredients are moistened. Stir in the coconut and raisins. Scrape the dough into a bowl. Cover and refrigerate overnight.

Preheat the oven to 325°F. Position racks in the upper and lower thirds of the oven.

For large cookies, scoop about 2 level tablespoons of dough and place the cookies about 3 inches apart on the cookie sheet. For small cookies, scoop 1 level tablespoon of dough. Bake for 15 to 17 minutes for large cookies, 13 to 15 minutes for small cookies, or until the cookies are deep golden brown. Rotate sheets from top to bottom and front to back about halfway through the baking time to ensure even baking. Use a metal pancake turner to transfer cookies to a rack to cool completely before storing or stacking. *May be stored, airtight, for several days.*

*Makes 40 3 1/4-inch cookies or 80 2 1/2-inch cookies*

**Ingredients**

1 cup plus 2 tablespoons all-purpose flour
2 cups rolled oats
3/4 teaspoon baking soda
1 teaspoon ground cinnamon
1/4 teaspoon ground nutmeg
16 tablespoons unsalted butter
3/4 cup (packed) brown sugar, lump free
3/4 cup granulated sugar
1 teaspoon vanilla extract
1/2 teaspoon salt
2 large eggs
3/4 cup unsweetened dried coconut (available at health food stores or by mail order)
1 cup raisins

**Equipment**

2 cookie sheets, greased

ı̇hought Moravian Spice Cookies were boring
til I tasted these perfectly spiced, crisp, tender
okies adapted from a recipe by Edna Lewis.
ıtience and a freezer are necessary to handle
s very soft dough successfully.

# ̇oravian Spice Cookies

ńbine the flour, baking powder, baking soda, salt, and spices in a medium
ẁl and mix together thoroughly with a whisk or fork. Set aside.

ıng the back of a large spoon in a large mixing bowl, mash the butter with the
ẁn sugar until well blended. Add the egg and mix until smooth. Mix in the
̇ ingredients, using your hands if necessary. Mix in the molasses. Divide the
ıgh into quarters and wrap airtight. Refrigerate at least 2 hours or overnight.

̇heat the oven to 375°F. with racks in the upper and lower thirds of the oven.

̇l one quarter of the dough a scant $1/8$ inch thick between 2 sheets of plastic
̇m a plastic bag (not wax paper). Slide a cookie sheet under the plastic sheets
̇d dough. Place in the freezer. Repeat with the remaining quarters. Remove
̇ first piece after 15 minutes or when the top sheet of plastic can be peeled
̇ easily. Cut cookies, leaving them on the bottom sheet of plastic. Return the
ıgh to the freezer. Repeat with the remaining dough. Working quickly, use a
̇n metal pancake turner to transfer cookies from the coldest piece of dough,
̇nch apart on the cookie sheets. When the cookies become too soft to move,
̇turn the dough to the freezer and remove another piece. Continue to fill
̇okie sheets. Save scraps to be rerolled. Bake cookies 8 to 9 minutes, or until
̇minute after they rise and fall. Rotate the sheets from back to front and upper
̇ lower halfway through the baking time to ensure even baking. Slide the pan
̇ers onto cooling racks. Cool cookies completely before stacking or storing.
̇ay be stored, airtight, for 3 to 4 weeks.

*Makes 7 dozen 2 1/2 - inch cookies*

## Ingredients

2$1/4$ cups all-purpose flour
1 teaspoon baking powder
$1/4$ teaspoon baking soda
$1/4$ teaspoon salt
1 teaspoon ground cinnamon
2 teaspoons ground ginger
$1/2$ teaspoon ground cloves
8 tablespoons unsalted butter,
   softened
1 $2/3$ cups (packed) dark brown
   sugar, lump free
1 large egg
$1/2$ cup light molasses

## Equipment

2 cookie sheets, lined with
   parchment paper or foil
2$1/2$-inch cookie cutter, round
   or any favorite shape

These are very spicy and loaded with diced crystalliz
Australian ginger. I especially like the crackly tops and t
possibility of controlling the ratio of chewy to crunch
My daughter is charmed by the smaller cookies, which a
also good company with a cup of coffe

# Ginger Snaps

...es 48 2 1/2-inch cookies or
3/4-inch cookies

**...redients**

...ps all-purpose flour
...aspoons baking soda
...aspoons ground ginger
...teaspoons ground
...innamon
...easpoon ground allspice
...easpoon salt
...blespoons unsalted butter,
...elted
...cup dark molasses
...cup granulated sugar
...cup (packed) light brown
...ugar, lump free
...rge egg
...cup finely chopped
...rystallized ginger
...2 2/3 ounces)
...out 1/4 cup additional
...ranulated sugar or coarse
...white sugar crystals, for
...olling the cookies

**...uipment**

...ookie sheets, lined with
...parchment paper or ungreased

Preheat the oven to 350°F. Position the racks in the upper and lower thirds of the oven, or in the center if you will bake only 1 sheet at a time.

Combine the flour, baking soda, ginger, cinnamon, allspice, and salt in a medium bowl and mix together thoroughly with a whisk or fork. Set aside.

Combine the warm (not hot) butter, molasses, granulated sugar, brown sugar, and the egg in a large bowl. Mix thoroughly. Add the flour mixture and crystallized ginger and stir until incorporated.

Form the dough into 1 1/4-inch balls (slightly more than 1 level tablespoon of dough) to make cookies 2 1/2 inches in diameter or use 1/2 tablespoon of dough to make 1 3/4-inch cookies. Roll dough balls in sugar and place them 2 inches apart on the cookie sheets. Bake for 10 to 12 minutes for large cookies, 8 to 10 minutes for small cookies, or until they puff up, crack on the surface, and then deflate in the oven. For chewier cookies, remove them from the oven when at least half of the cookies have begun to deflate; for crunchier edges with chewy centers, bake a minute or so longer. Rotate the sheets from back to front and top to bottom about halfway through the baking time to ensure even baking.

Slide the parchment liners onto racks or use a metal pancake turner to transfer the cookies from the pan. Cool completely before stacking or storing. Cookies served on the day they are baked will be chewy with crunchy edges. Ginger Snaps become completely chewy stored in an airtight container. They are best eaten within 3 days.

almond biscotti
82

cornmeal and fruit biscotti
84

martha's tender mandelbrodt
85

orange-chocolate chip biscotti
86

chocolate biscotti
89

cotti have become as American as apple pie and infinitely more ubiquitous. Café-goers who invest ularly in single biscotti will be astonished at how easy they are to make. How did a twice-baked, dry-bones, anise-flavored Italian cookie—so crunchy that it begs to be splashed in sweet wine or strong fee—acquire American citizenship? Probably by losing its anise-flavored accent and welcoming a riad of flavorful chunks and chips, from chocolate to cherries in addition to any nut in the universe or nuts at all. Not all biscotti are even so hard and dry; I've included a texture to suit everyone, from per crunchy to something best described as a satisfying slice of crumbly toasted cake.

# Biscotti

## Here's what I learned

...Each recipe for biscotti has a distinctive texture depending on the proportion of ingredients, number of eggs, amount of butter or oil (if any), and type of leavening.

...You may create endless variations by substituting nuts (toasted or untoasted), dried or candied fruits, and liqueurs. You may add chocolate chips, or even ground coffee beans, or citrus zest. You may exchange brown sugar or maple sugar with equal amounts of granulated sugar, and experiment with spices such as cinnamon, clove, nutmeg, cardamom, and ginger.

...Although you may slice the loaf of biscotti and rebake the cookies after as little as 5 to 10 minutes of cooling, you may also wait to perform these steps at your convenience.

...Shape dough into a short wide loaf to make long, thin, elegant biscotti or shape long narrow loaves to make shorter, fatter biscotti; the first baking time will not be affected. You may also slice biscotti as thick or as thin as you like, so long as you adjust the second baking time accordingly.

...The driest, crunchiest biscotti will keep for several weeks in an airtight tin.

...Dried or candied fruits are best in the softer, cakier style of biscotti, which are best consumed within a week or two.

I tasted these superb cookies in the kitchen of Carole Tibor
cooking school director at Jungle Jim's in Cincinnati, Oh
I am partial to this style of biscotti with its porous, hard, crunc
texture. Although they are eminently dippable (in espresso
dessert wine), I love them bone dry, loud, and crunch

# Almond Biscotti

Preheat the oven to 300°F. Position a rack in the middle of the oven.

Combine the flour, sugar, baking powder, and salt in a medium bowl and mix together thoroughly with a whisk or a fork. Set aside.

Whisk the eggs, amaretto, vanilla, and anise extract, if using, in a large bowl until well blended. Stir in the flour mixture and then the almonds. The dough will be thick and sticky. Scrape the dough into a long log shape lengthwise on the cookie sheet. Flour your hands and shape the dough into a long flat loaf about 10 inches long and 5 inches wide.

Bake until firm and dry, about 50 minutes. Remove from the oven and let cool for about 10 minutes. Transfer the loaf carefully to a cutting board. Using a long serrated knife, cut the loaf on the diagonal into slices 1/2 inch wide. Lay the slices, cut side down, on the cookie sheet. Bake for 20 minutes; turn each cookie over and bake for 15 to 20 minutes more, or until the cookies are golden brown. Place the cookie sheet on a rack to cool. Cool cookies completely before stacking or storing. *May be stored, airtight, for several weeks.*

*Makes about 20 biscotti*

**Ingredients**

2 cups all-purpose flour
1 cup sugar
1 teaspoon baking powder
1/8 teaspoon salt
3 large eggs
2 tablespoons amaretto liqueur
   or 2 tablespoons rum with
   1 teaspoon almond extract
1 teaspoon vanilla extract
1 teaspoon anise extract
   (optional)
1 cup whole almonds,
   toasted and chopped

**Equipment**

Cookie sheet, lined with
   parchment paper or greased
   and floured

### Variations

**Hazelnut Biscotti:** Use Frangelico liqueur instead of amaretto and toasted and skinned hazelnuts (see page 111) instead of almonds.

**Chocolate Chip Biscotti:** Omit liqueur and anise extract. Substitute 1/2 cup brown sugar for 1/2 cup of the granulated sugar. Substitute 2/3 cup chopped walnuts and 2/3 cup chocolate chips for the almonds.

**Orange and Almond Biscotti:** Omit liqueur and anise extract. Substitute 1/4 teaspoon orange extract, grated zest of a medium orange, and 2 tablespoons orange juice.

# Cornmeal and Fruit Biscotti

Preheat the oven to 350°F. Position a rack in the middle of the oven.

Combine the flour, cornmeal, baking powder, and salt in a medium bowl and mix together thoroughly with a whisk or fork. Set aside.

Beat the butter and sugar in a large bowl with an electric mixer until blended. Add the eggs, vanilla, and lemon zest, and beat until light and fluffy.

Add the flour mixture, stirring until all of the ingredients are moistened. Add the raisins, mixing with your hands if necessary. Shape the dough into a 12 X 2-inch log and place it on the cookie sheet.

Bake for 35 to 40 minutes, or until lightly browned and cracked on top. Cool for 5 to 10 minutes. Transfer the loaf carefully to a cutting board. Using a long serrated knife, cut the loaf on the diagonal into slices about 3/8 inch wide. Lay the slices, cut side down, on the cookie sheet. Bake for about 10 minutes, or until the cookies are barely beginning to brown at the edges. Set the pan on a rack. Cool the cookies completely before stacking or storing. *May be stored, airtight, for at least 2 weeks.*

*Makes about 30 biscotti*

### Ingredients

1 cup all-purpose flour
1 cup cornmeal
1/2 teaspoon baking powder
1/4 teaspoon salt
4 tablespoons unsalted butter, softened
1 cup sugar
2 large eggs
1 teaspoon vanilla extract
1 teaspoon finely grated lemon zest
1 cup raisins or dried cherries, cranberries, or blueberries, or chopped dried apricots

### Equipment

Cookie sheet, lined with parchment paper or greased and floured

My grandmother Mabel's sister Martha was a talented home cook and baker. Her grandsons are the New York chef/restaurateurs Eric and Bruce Bromberg. They studied in France, but were influenced by Martha. She, in turn, credits her mother, the most gifted baker of all and the true source of our family talent.

# Martha's Tender Mandelbrodt

Preheat the oven to 350°F. Position racks in lower and upper thirds of the oven.

Combine the Wondra flour and baking powder in a bowl and whisk together thoroughly. Set aside.

Beat the eggs, sugar, vanilla, and zest in a large bowl with an electric mixer for 4 to 5 minutes, or until light and thick. Beat in the oil. Stir in the flour mixture, then the almonds. Batter will be thin. Scrape the batter out in 2 long strips down the full length of the jelly-roll pan. Batter will flow considerably. Use a rubber spatula to neaten and separate the 2 strips of batter.

Bake for 30 minutes on the lower oven rack. Remove the pan and reduce the oven temperature to 325°F. Cool the loaves for 5 or 10 minutes on the pan. Turn the foil liner over, with the long flat loaves still attached. Peel the foil from the bottom of the loaves. Transfer the loaves, right side up, to a cutting board. Use a serrated knife to cut each loaf on the diagonal into slices 3/4 inch wide. Lay the slices, cut side down, dividing them between 2 cookie sheets. Bake the slices at 325°F. for 12 to 15 minutes, or until golden brown. Rotate sheets from front to back and top to bottom halfway through the baking time to ensure even baking. Turn each slice over and bake for 12 to 15 minutes more, until golden brown. Rotate cookie sheets as before. Cool cookies completely before storing. *May be stored, airtight, for several weeks.*

*Makes 44 cookies*

### Ingredients
2 cups Wondra flour
1 teaspoon baking powder
4 large eggs
1 cup sugar
1 teaspoon vanilla extract
Finely grated zest of 1 lemon
   or orange
1/4 cup corn oil
1/2 cup slivered almonds

### Equipment
17 X 11-inch jelly-roll pan,
   lined with foil
2 cookie sheets, ungreased

*Wondra flour is a quick-mixing combination of wheat and malted barley made by Gold Medal. It comes in a slim cylindrical box.*

These super crunchy biscotti are quite low in fat, leaving ple[n] of room in the fat budget for chocolate chips. This is like havin[g] salad for dinner in order to enjoy a hot fudge sundae for desse[rt]. Please do not ruin this delicious cookie by substituting lo[w] or reduced-fat chocolate chips for the real thing. The point is [to] use the best and most flavorful chocolate chips. You might ev[en] try one of the "gourmet" bittersweet chocolate chips— they are bigger, smoother, and more adu[lt].

# Orange-Chocolate Chip Biscotti

Preheat the oven to 300°F. Position the rack in the middle of the oven.

Combine the flour, baking soda, and salt in a small bowl and mix together thoroughly with a whisk or fork.

Whisk the eggs, sugar, vanilla, orange extract, and zest in a medium mixing bowl until well blended. Mix in the orange juice. Using a rubber spatula or wooden spoon, stir in the flour mixture just until combined. Stir in the chocolate chips. The batter will be thick and sticky. Scrape the batter onto the baking sheet, dividing it evenly into 2 long skinny loaves, about 14 inches long and 2 to $2^{1}/_2$ inches wide. Loaves should be at least $2^{1}/_2$ inches apart. Neaten the edges of each loaf with a spatula.

Bake for 35 minutes, or until firm but springy when pressed with your fingers. Let cool for 10 minutes on the pan. Leave the oven turned on. Use both hands to remove each loaf carefully from the paper to a cutting board.

*Makes about 45 small biscotti*

**Ingredients**

$1^{2}/_3$ cups all-purpose flour
$^{1}/_2$ teaspoon baking soda
$^{1}/_4$ teaspoon salt
2 large eggs
$^{3}/_4$ cup sugar
1 teaspoon vanilla extract
$^{1}/_4$ teaspoon orange extract
Grated zest of $^{2}/_3$ medium orang[e]
2 tablespoons fresh orange juic[e]
1 cup semisweet chocolate chi[ps]

**Equipment**

Large heavy baking sheet, lined
  with parchment or wax paper
  or aluminum foil

ng a sharp serrated knife, slice loaves on the diagonal into 1/2-inch slices.
 the biscotti, cut side down, on the baking sheet. Bake for 12 minutes.
 the biscotti over and bake for 12 to 15 minutes more, or until golden
wn. Place the baking sheet on a rack to cool. Cool the biscotti completely
ore stacking or storing. The flavor develops and the biscotti become
 e tender after 2 or 3 days stored in an airtight container. *May be stored,*
*ght, at room temperature for several weeks.*

**iation**

colate Chip Biscotti: The quintessential American biscotti. They taste
 ctly like super crunchy chocolate chip cookies.

duce the amount of sugar to 1/4 cup plus 2 tablespoons and add an equal
 antity of brown sugar. Omit the orange extract, orange zest, and orange
 e. Reduce the quantity of chocolate chips to 2/3 cup and add 1/2 cup
 pped walnuts.

*If you wish to reduce the
fat in this cookie more
than I already have,
cut back on the quantity
(not the quality) of the
chocolate. To make
less go farther, chop
the chips into smaller
pieces or use mini chips.
Make these at least
one day ahead.*

These dry crunchy biscotti have a denser, less open grain than the Almond Biscotti. The deep cocoa flavor is satisfying and not too sweet.

# Chocolate Biscotti

Preheat the oven to 300°F. Position a rack in the middle of the oven.

Combine the flour, cocoa, espresso powder, baking powder, and salt in a medium bowl and mix together thoroughly with a whisk or fork. Set aside.

Using the back of a large spoon, in a mixing bowl or with a mixer, beat the butter and sugar together until soft and creamy. Mix in the eggs and vanilla. Add the flour mixture and stir just until all the ingredients are moistened. Add the walnuts, mixing with your hands, if necessary. Divide the dough in half. Shape each half into a long, flat oblong loaf, about 10 inches long, 4 inches wide, and 3/4 inch high on the cookie sheet.

Bake for 35 to 40 minutes, or until a toothpick inserted in the center comes out dry. Cool for 5 to 10 minutes. Transfer the loaf carefully to a cutting board. Using a long serrated knife, cut the loaf on the diagonal into slices about 3/8 inch wide. Lay the slices, cut side down, on the cookie sheet. Bake for 30 to 35 minutes, or until the surface of the cookies feels dry and crusty. Place the cookie sheet on a rack and cool the cookies completely before stacking or storing. *May be stored, airtight, for several weeks.*

## Variations

**Chocolate-Orange Biscotti:** Add 1 tablespoon finely grated orange zest with the vanilla.

**Chocolate-Hazelnut Biscotti:** Substitute hazelnuts, toasted and skinned (see page 111) then chopped, for the walnuts and add 1 tablespoon Frangelico liqueur with the vanilla.

**Mocha Latte or Mocha Espresso Biscotti:** Omit the walnuts and substitute milk chocolate or semisweet chocolate chips and 2 tablespoons coarsely ground espresso beans.

---

*kes about 36 biscotti*

**redients**

ups all-purpose flour
cup unsweetened Dutch
rocess cocoa powder,
referably imported
aspoons instant espresso
r coffee powder
aspoons baking powder
easpoon salt
blespoons unsalted butter,
oftened
up sugar
rge eggs
aspoons vanilla extract
up walnuts, coarsely chopped

**uipment**

okie sheet, lined with
archment paper or greased
and floured

turtle bars
109

toffee bars
108

rocky road bars
107

fruit and nut bars
105

chewy almond and
cherry bars
104

apricot-lemon bars
102

new classic brownies
93

bittersweet brownies
96

very fudgey brownie:
97

espresso swirl brown
98

blondies
100

lemon bars
101

bister than cookies, denser than cake, brownies and bars are quicker and easier than either, while
ering the best of both. My favorites have multiple textures: crusty brownies with creamy centers,
unchy but gooey Lemon Bars, chunky and chewy Fruit and Nut Bars. In the bargain, there is no lengthy
ating, delicate folding, or individual shaping. Brownies and bars never fall (unless they are supposed to)
d an extra minute in the oven isn't the end of the world. When there's not enough time to mix and
eside over a batch of cookies (in and out of the oven every ten minutes), chances are you can manage
slide a pan of Blondies in the oven and still take a shower while they bake. If need be, transport them
the party in the pan.

# Brownies and Bars

### Here's what I learned

…Brownies and bars baked in a foil-lined pan are a breeze to unmold and transfer before cutting into neat squares or rectangles. The downside is that you'll never again be forced to eat that first deformed brownie that stuck in the corner of the pan.

…Lined pans are easier to clean and never suffer knife scars from cutting in the pan.

…Fully lined pans prevent wet or gooey toppings, like lemon or caramel, from flowing under the crust and/or sticking to the sides of the pan.

…To line a pan with foil the easy way, turn the pan upside down on the counter. Center a 12-inch square of foil over the pan. Fold the edges of the foil down over the four sides of the pan, folding the corners neatly as though wrapping a package. Slip the foil off the pan. Turn the pan right side up and press the foil into the pan, smoothing it across the bottom, into the corners, and up the sides.

After much fooling around with brownie recipes, I like this one. The ingredient proportions are exactly those of Marion Cunningham's from her wonderful *Fannie Farmer Baking Book* but the technique (see the Steve Ritual, page 95) is different and rather magical.

# New Classic Brownies

Preheat the oven to 400°F. Position a rack in the lower third of the oven.

Melt the butter with the chocolate in the top of a double boiler or in a medium heatproof bowl set in a pan of barely simmering water. Stir frequently until the mixture is melted and smooth.

Remove the top of the double boiler (or the bowl) from the heat. Stir in the sugar, vanilla, and salt. Add the eggs, one at a time, stirring until each is incorporated before adding the next. Stir in the flour and beat with a wooden spoon until the batter is smooth and glossy and comes away from the sides of the pan, about 1 minute. Stir in the nuts, if using. Scrape the batter into the pan. Bake for 20 minutes, or until the brownies just begin to pull away from the sides of the pan. The surface of the brownies will look dry but a toothpick inserted in the center will still be quite gooey.

While the brownies are baking, prepare an ice bath: Fill a roasting pan or large baking pan with ice cubes and water about 3/4 inch deep. (Trust me on this—it's the crucial component of the Steve Ritual. Just turn to page 95 for proof and instructions.)

When the brownies are ready, remove the pan from the oven and set it immediately in the ice bath, taking care not to splash water on the brownies. Cool the brownies in the ice bath.

When cool, slide a knife between the pan and the brownies on the unlined sides. Lift the ends of the parchment or foil liner and transfer the brownies to a cutting board. Cut into 16 squares. *May be stored, airtight, for 2 to 3 days.*

*(continued)*

kes 16 brownies

**gredients**

ablespoons unsalted butter
unces unsweetened chocolate
/4 cups sugar
easpoon vanilla extract
teaspoon salt
arge eggs
cup all-purpose flour
cup walnut or pecan
pieces (optional)

**quipment**

inch square metal pan,
lined across the bottom and
up 2 opposite sides with
parchment paper or foil

À la Mode

### The Steve Ritual

When Maya Klein, my assistant, told me about the Steve Ritual—which calls for baking brownies for only about twenty minutes at 400°F. and then cooling them in an ice bath—she said it originated when her husband (Steve) was in college and one of his college roommates discovered that the oven was way too hot or possibly on fire and the brownies were in mortal danger. Without thinking to save himself, the smart roommate (she thinks it was Steve) rescued the brownies by shoving them into the freezer next to a frozen pizza, which arrested the cooking instantly and produced, by accident, brownies divinely moist and creamy inside yet crusty and satisfying on the outside.

In an eloquent full-page single-spaced document, Steve himself claimed that the ritual evolved slowly and thoughtfully, requiring a rigorous application of the scientific method and pushing his analytical and baking skills to the very limit over the course of many months. By the time the ritual was perfected, he said that he and his roommates had taken to dimming the lights in the kitchen before retrieving the brownies from the freezer—and here Steve would close his own eyes—for fear of giving the secret away!

I don't know which story is true. But I do know that brownies with at least 1/2 cup of flour (for an 8-inch brownie pan), even cakey brownies, even brownie mixes, turn out more luscious and decadent when made with the Steve Ritual. (Brownies with less than 1/2 cup of flour and more than 5 ounces of chocolate are already so gooey that the Steve Ritual is unnecessary.)

New Classic Brownies (page 93) tested with the Steve Ritual won hands down against the same recipe baked in a conventional manner. Not only was the crust crustier and the center creamier, but the flavor was livelier and more chocolatey as well! Fortunately a pan of ice water is a perfect substitute for the freezer in the original story. The frozen pizza is optional.

# Bittersweet Brownies

Richer and even more chocolatey than New Classic Brownies . . .

Preheat the oven to 325°F. Position a rack in the lower third of the oven.

Melt the butter with all the chocolate in the top of a double boiler or in a medium heatproof bowl set in a pan of barely simmering water. Stir frequently until the mixture is melted and smooth. Remove the top of the double boiler (or the bowl) from the heat. Stir in the sugar, salt, and vanilla. Add the eggs, one at a time, stirring until each is incorporated before adding the next. Stir in the flour and beat with a wooden spoon until the batter is smooth and glossy and comes away from the sides of the pan, about 1 minute. Stir in the nuts if using. Scrape the batter into the pan.

Bake for 35 to 40 minutes, or until the brownies just begin to pull away from the sides of the pan. Cool on a rack for at least 1 hour before removing from the pan. Slide a knife between the pan and the brownies on the unlined sides. Lift the parchment or foil ends to transfer the brownies to a cutting board. Cut into 16 squares. *May be stored, airtight, for 2 to 3 days.*

## Variation

Extra Bittersweet Scharffen Berger Brownies: Chocolate sophisticates will be aware of the new imported and domestic bittersweet chocolates available in specialty food shops. These bars, labeled *70%*, contain more chocolate (70 percent) and less sugar (30 percent) than typical semisweet or bittersweet chocolates, which are about 50 percent chocolate and 50 percent sugar. Robert Steinberg, chocolate maker and coproprietor of Scharffen Berger Chocolate Maker, created this brownie recipe especially for his Scharffen Berger 70% chocolate.

Prepare Bittersweet Brownies, substituting 8 ounces of 70% chocolate for the 3 ounces unsweetened and 3 ounces semisweet chocolate in the recipe.

*Makes 16 brownies*

**Ingredients**

6 tablespoons unsalted butter
3 ounces unsweetened chocolate, coarsely chopped
3 ounces semisweet or bittersweet chocolate, coarsely chopped
1 cup sugar
1/4 teaspoon salt
1/2 teaspoon vanilla extract
2 large eggs
1/4 cup all-purpose flour
2/3 cup walnut or pecan pieces (optional)

**Equipment**

8-inch square pan, lined across the bottom and up 2 opposite sides with parchment paper or foil

...eat brownies with less fat? These will fool you. To
...ke them taste and feel as rich and gooey as they
...n be, remember that even the richest brownies
...y out when overbaked. With less fat, *you must
absolutely positively* remove the brownies from the
...en when the toothpick is still a little gooey.
...mbining cocoa with sizzling hot butter brings
...t the deepest chocolate flavor.

## ...ery Fudgey Brownies

...heat the oven to 350°F. Position a rack in the lower third of the oven.

...a small bowl, mix the flour, baking powder, and salt together thoroughly
...h a whisk or fork.

...a medium saucepan, heat the butter until melted and sizzling hot. Remove
...m the heat and stir in the cocoa. Stir in the sugars. The mixture will look like
...mass of very dark brown sugar. Add the egg, egg whites, and vanilla. Stir
...skly, about 40 strokes, until smooth. Add the flour mixture. Stir until incorpo-
...ed and smooth, 40 to 50 strokes. Scrape the batter into the pan and spread
...level. The batter will be very shallow in the pan.

...ke 15 to 18 minutes or until a toothpick inserted in the center comes out
...th a little batter—thickened and gooey, not thin and liquid—still clinging to
... Do not overbake. Cool on a rack. Slide a knife along the unlined edges of
...e pan. Lift the ends of the pan liner and transfer the brownies to a cutting
...ard. Cut into 16 squares. If you have not overbaked the brownies, they will
...main moist and delicious for at least 2 days in an airtight container.

*Makes 16 2-inch brownies*

### Ingredients

3/4 cup all-purpose flour
1/4 teaspoon baking powder
1/4 teaspoon salt
4 1/2 tablespoons unsalted butter
1/2 cup plus 1 tablespoon
    unsweetened nonalkalized
    cocoa (not Dutch process or
    European style)
3/4 cup granulated sugar
1/3 cup (packed) light brown
    sugar, lump free
1 large egg
2 large egg whites
2 teaspoons vanilla

### Equipment

8-inch square pan, lined across
    the bottom and 2 opposite sides
    with parchment paper or foil

Adult brownies. A jolt of strong espresso flavor, bar[e]
sweetened, makes a suave creamy complement to bitterswe[et]
bars. I don't use the Steve Ritual (see page 95) for the[se]
brownies because the moist gooey espresso mixture is mo[re]
luxurious in contrast with a slightly cakier brown[ie.]

# Espresso Swirl Brownies

Preheat the oven to 325°F. Position a rack in the lower third of the oven.

Mix the batter for New Classic Brownies. Spread all but 1/2 cup of the batter in the prepared pan. Set aside.

Combine the coffee powder with the water. Set aside. Mix the cream cheese with the sugar and vanilla until smooth. Stir in the egg and the coffee mixture until well blended. Spread the cream cheese mixture over the batter in the pan. Spoon dollops of reserved brownie batter on top. Without scraping the bottom of the pan, draw a table knife through the dollops to swirl and marble the chocolate and espresso batter without thoroughly mixing them.

Bake for 20 to 25 minutes, or until the brownies just begin to pull away from the sides of the pan. Cool on a rack. Refrigerate and chill thoroughly before cutting, about 2 hours.

Slide a knife between the pan and the brownies on the unlined sides. Lift the ends of the parchment or foil liner and transfer the brownies to a cutting board. Cut into 16 squares. *May be stored, airtight, in the refrigerator for 4 to 5 days.*

*Makes 16 brownies*

**Ingredients**

Ingredients for New Classic Brownies (page 93), without the nuts
1 tablespoon instant coffee or espresso powder
1 tablespoon water
8 ounces cream cheese, softened
1/3 cup sugar
1 teaspoon vanilla extract
1 large egg

**Equipment**

9-inch square pan, lined across the bottom and up 2 opposite sides with parchment paper or foil

# Blondies

Preheat the oven to 350°F. Position a rack in the lower third of the oven.

Combine the flour, baking powder, and salt in a small bowl and mix together thoroughly with a whisk or fork. Set aside.

Melt the butter in a small saucepan. Remove the pan from the heat and stir in the brown sugar. Use a wooden spoon to beat in the egg, vanilla, and rum, if using. Stir in the flour mixture followed by half of the walnuts. Spread the batter in the pan. Sprinkle the remaining walnuts and the chocolate chips evenly over the top.

Bake for 20 to 25 minutes, or until the nuts look toasted, the top is golden brown, and the edges have pulled away from the sides of the pan. Cool in the pan on a rack. Lift the ends of the parchment or foil and transfer to a cutting board. Use a long sharp knife to cut into 16 squares. *May be stored, airtight, for 3 to 4 days.*

*Makes 16 blondies*

**Ingredients**

1 cup all-purpose flour
3/4 teaspoon baking powder
1/8 teaspoon salt
8 tablespoons unsalted butter
1 cup (packed) light brown sugar, lump free
1 large egg
1/2 teaspoon vanilla extract
1 tablespoon dark rum or bourbon (optional)
2/3 cup walnut pieces
1/2 cup semisweet chocolate chips

**Equipment**

8-inch square pan, lined across the bottom and up 2 opposite sides with parchment paper or foil

...s of luscious tangy topping on a buttery shortbread ...st. Lemon bars are an indulgent snack on their ...n, but I also like to cut them in half and arrange ...m on a platter with half-size brownies or Beacon ... Cookies (page 56). Then it's dessert.

# ...mon Bars

...heat the oven to 350°F. Position a rack in the lower third of the oven.

...make the crust: Cut butter into chunks and melt it in a medium saucepan ...r medium heat. Remove from the heat and stir in the sugar, vanilla, and ... Add the flour and mix just until incorporated. Press the dough evenly over ... bottom of the pan. Bake for 25 to 30 minutes, or until the crust is well ...wned at the edges and lightly browned in the center.

...make the topping: While the crust is baking, stir together the sugar and ...ur in a medium bowl until well mixed. Whisk in the eggs. Stir in the lemon ...t and juice. When the crust is ready, turn the oven down to 300°F. and slide ... rack out without removing the pan. Pour the filling over the hot crust.

...ke for 20 to 25 minutes, or until the topping is puffed at the edges and no ...ger jiggles in the center when the pan is tapped. Set on a rack to cool com- ...tely in the pan. Lift the ends of the foil liner and transfer to a cutting board. ...e a long sharp knife to cut into sixteen 2-inch bars. *May be stored, airtight,* ...*the refrigerator.* Lemon Bars keep perfectly for about 3 days; after 3 days ... crust softens but the bars still taste quite good for the remainder of a ...eek. Do not freeze. Sieve powdered sugar over the bars just before serving.

*Makes 16 2-inch bars*

### Ingredients

Crust:
8 tablespoons unsalted butter, softened
1/4 cup granulated sugar
3/4 teaspoon vanilla extract
1/8 teaspoon salt
1 cup all-purpose flour

Topping:
1 cup plus 2 tablespoons sugar
3 tablespoons all-purpose flour
3 large eggs
1 1/2 teaspoons finely grated lemon zest
1/2 cup strained fresh lemon juice
2 to 3 tablespoons powdered sugar, for dusting

### Equipment

8-inch square pan, lined on the bottom and up all 4 sides with foil

The name says it. Lemon bar lovers
add these to the repertoire. I like them b
with a toasted hazelnut cru

# Apricot-Lemon Bars

Preheat the oven to 350°F. Position a rack in the lower third of the oven.

To make the crust: Cut butter into chunks and melt it in a medium saucepan over medium heat. Remove from the heat and stir in the sugar, vanilla, and salt. Add the flour and mix just until incorporated. Press the dough evenly over the bottom of the pan. Bake for 25 to 30 minutes, or until the crust is well browned at the edges and lightly browned in the center.

To make the topping: While the crust is baking, stir together the sugar and flour in a medium bowl until well mixed. Whisk in the eggs. Stir in the pre- serves, breaking up any extra large pieces. Mix in the lemon juice. When the crust is ready, turn the oven down to 300°F. and slide the rack out without removing the pan. Pour the filling over the hot crust.

Bake for 20 to 25 minutes, or until the topping is puffed at the edges and no longer jiggles in the center when the pan is tapped. Set on a rack to cool completely in the pan. Lift the foil liner and transfer to a cutting board. Use a long sharp knife to cut sixteen 2-inch bars. *May be stored, airtight, in the refrigerator.* Apricot-Lemon Bars keep perfectly for about 3 days; after 3 days the crust softens but the bars still taste quite good for the remainder of a week. Do not freeze. Sieve powdered sugar over the bars just before serving.

*Makes 16 2-inch bars*

**Ingredients**

Crust:
8 tablespoons unsalted butter,
   softened
1/4 cup granulated sugar
3/4 teaspoon vanilla extract
1/8 teaspoon salt
1 cup all-purpose flour

Topping:
1/4 cup sugar
2 tablespoons all-purpose flour
2 large eggs
1/2 cup apricot preserves
1/3 cup strained fresh lemon jui
2 to 3 tablespoons powdered
   sugar, for dusting

**Equipment**

8-inch square pan, lined on the
   bottom and all 4 sides with fo

**Variation**

**Nut Crust for Apricot-Lemon Bars:** Decrease the flour by 3 tablespoons. Put the flour with the sugar, salt, and 1/4 cup almonds or toasted and skinned hazelnuts (see page 111) in a food processor fitted with a steel blade. Pulse until the nuts are finely ground. Add the melted butter and pulse just until the dry ingredients look damp and the mixture begins to clump around the blade. Remove the dough from the processor and knead it a few times until smooth. Proceed with the recipe.

# Chewy Almond and Cherry Bars

Preheat the oven to 350°F. Position a rack in the lower third of the oven.

Process the almonds with the flour in a food processor fitted with a steel blade until the almonds are finely ground. Add the salt and baking powder and pulse to mix. Set aside.

Melt the butter in a medium saucepan. Remove from the heat and stir in the sugar. Using a wooden spoon, beat in the egg and almond extract. Stir in the flour mixture, followed by the dried fruit. Spread the batter evenly in the pan.

Bake for 20 to 25 minutes, or until the edges are golden brown and have pulled away from the sides of the pan and the top is light golden brown. Cool in the pan on a rack. Run a knife along the unlined sides of the pan. Lift the ends of the paper or foil liner and transfer to a cutting board. Use a long sharp knife to cut into 16 squares. *May be stored, airtight, for at least 1 week.*

*Makes 16 bars*

**Ingredients**

3/4 cup whole almonds, with
    or without skins
1 cup all-purpose flour
1/8 teaspoon salt
3/4 teaspoon baking powder
8 tablespoons unsalted butter
3/4 cup plus 2 tablespoons sug.
1 large egg
1/4 teaspoon almond extract
1/2 cup dried tart cherries,
    preferably Montmorency, or
    dried cranberries or choppe
    dried apricots

**Equipment**

8-inch square pan, lined across
    the bottom and up 2 opposite
    sides with parchment paper
    or foil

sy. Lots of dried fruit and nuts and with just enough
tter to hold everything together. The results are not
ly chewy, crunchy, and delicious but also healthy.
eate endless variations by substituting combinations
dried cranberries or cherries, dried pears, whole
monds or hazelnuts.

# ruit and Nut Bars

heat the oven to 325°F. Position the rack in the center of the oven.

mbine the flour, baking soda, baking powder, and salt in a large bowl and
k together thoroughly. Add the brown sugar, walnuts, dates, and apricots.
e your fingers to mix the ingredients until nuts and fruits are coated with
e flour mixture, separating any sticky fruit pieces.

at the egg with the vanilla in a small bowl until light colored and thick.
rape the egg into the large bowl and mix with your hands until all of the fruit
d nut pieces are thinly coated with batter. Spread the mixture in the pan,
essing to even it out.

ke for 35 to 40 minutes, or until the thin batter coating is golden brown and
s pulled away from the sides of the pan. Cool in the pan on a rack. Run a
nall knife around the unlined edges of the pan. Lift the ends of the paper or
l liner and transfer to a cutting board. Use a sharp knife to cut 16 squares.
ay be stored, airtight, for at least 2 weeks at room temperature, longer in
e refrigerator.

*Makes 16 bars*

### Ingredients

1/4 cup plus 2 tablespoons
    all-purpose flour
1/8 teaspoon baking soda
1/8 teaspoon baking powder
1/4 teaspoon salt
1/4 cup plus 2 tablespoons
    (packed) light or dark brown
    sugar, lump free
2 cups walnut pieces
1 1/2 cups dates, pits removed and
    cut into quarters
1 cup (lightly packed) dried
    apricot halves, each cut in half
1 large egg
1/2 teaspoon vanilla extract

### Equipment

8-inch square pan, lined across
    the bottom and up 2 opposite
    sides with parchment paper
    or foil

This is a no-brainer. Try it on friends w[ho]
think they are too sophisticated [to]
appreciate chocolate with marshmallo[ws]
and nuts on a graham cracker cru[st.]

# ocky Road Bars

heat the oven to 350°F. Position the oven rack in the lower third of the
n.

ng a fork, mix the butter with the graham cracker crumbs and sugar until
of the crumbs are moistened. Turn the mixture into the pan and spread it
nly, pressing very firmly all over the bottom to form a crust. Scatter the
pieces evenly over the crust.

e for 10 minutes, or until the crust begins to turn golden brown. Remove
m the oven and scatter marshmallows and chocolate chips evenly over the
nuts. Return the pan to the oven for 10 to 12 minutes, or until the marsh-
llows are soft, barely golden, and merged with one another. Set on a rack
ool completely. Run a knife along the unlined sides of the pan. Lift the
ds of the foil liner and transfer the bars to a cutting board. Use a long sharp
fe to cut into sixteen 2-inch bars. *May be stored, airtight, for 4 to 5 days.*

*Makes 16 2-inch bars*

**Ingredients**

6 tablespoons unsalted butter,
   melted
1 1/2 cups fine graham cracker
   crumbs (made from 11 double
   graham crackers)
1/4 cup sugar
1 cup walnut pieces
2 cups miniature or quartered
   regular marshmallows
1 cup milk chocolate or
   semisweet chocolate chips

**Equipment**

8-inch square pan, lined across
   the bottom and up 2 opposite
   sides with foil

# Toffee Bars

Preheat the oven to 350°F. Position a rack in the lower third of the oven.

To make the shortbread: Cut butter into chunks and melt it in a medium saucepan over medium heat. Remove from the heat and stir in the brown sugar, vanilla, and salt. Add the flour and mix just until incorporated.

Bake for 20 to 25 minutes, or until well browned at the edges and golden brown in the center.

To make the topping: Sprinkle the hot crust with chocolate and return to the oven for 1 to 2 minutes, or just until the chocolate softens. Remove the pan from the oven and spread the chocolate evenly with the back of a spoon. Sprinkle the nuts over the chocolate. Set on a rack to cool. Lift the edges of the foil liner to transfer to a cutting board. Use a sharp knife to cut into 16 squares. *May be stored, airtight, for at least 1 month.*

*Makes 16 2-inch bars*

### Ingredients

Shortbread:
8 tablespoons unsalted butter
1/2 cup (packed) light brown su
1 teaspoon vanilla extract
1/8 teaspoon salt
1 cup all-purpose flour

Topping:
6 ounces milk or semisweet
chocolate, cut into small
pieces, or 1 cup chocolate
chips
1/2 cup chopped toasted almon

### Equipment

8-inch square pan, lined on
the bottom and up all 4 sides
with foil

y friend Beryl Radin's Aunt Florence gave us this
pecially rich and happy marriage of American flavors
gooey chewy caramel, pecans, and milk chocolate
a shortbread crust. The secret is to toast pecans on
e crust before adding the caramel topping. For the
st luxurious rendition, chop up a good-quality milk
ocolate bar in lieu of milk chocolate chips.

# urtle Bars

eheat the oven to 350°F. Position a rack in the lower third of the oven.

make the crust: Cut butter into chunks and melt it in a large saucepan over
edium heat. Remove from the heat and stir in the sugar, vanilla, and salt.
d the flour and mix just until incorporated. Press the dough evenly over the
ttom of the pan. Scatter the pecans over the dough.

ke until the pecans are lightly toasted, 10 to 12 minutes. Set the pan aside
t leave the oven on while making the topping.

make the topping: Combine the butter and brown sugar in a small
ucepan. Bring the mixture to a boil over medium heat, stirring occasionally.
il for 1 minute (mixture may look curdled). Pour the hot butter mixture over
e pecans on the crust. Bake for 15 to 18 minutes, or until the topping is dark
d bubbling vigorously. Remove the pan from the oven and scatter the choco-
te chips or chopped chocolate evenly over the top. (Or melt and drizzle the
ocolate decoratively over the bars after they have cooled.) Cool the bars in
e pan on a rack. Run a slim knife along the unlined sides of the pan. Lift the
ds of the foil liner and transfer to a cutting board. Use a long sharp knife
cut into 24 bars. *May be stored, airtight, for at least 1 week.*

*Makes 24 bars*

**Ingredients**

Crust:
12 tablespoons unsalted butter
1/3 cup granulated sugar
1 teaspoon vanilla extract
1/4 teaspoon salt
2 cups all-purpose flour
2 cups pecan halves

Topping:
8 tablespoons unsalted butter
3/4 cup (packed) light brown
    sugar, lump free
1 cup milk chocolate chips or
    6 ounces milk chocolate,
    chopped

**Equipment**

13 X 9-inch pan, lined on the
    bottom and all 4 sides with foil

# Ingredients

Cookie dough is not a fountain of youth or your grandmother's stockpot. Don't even consider using up your petrified dried fruit, old currants, slightly stale nuts, old spices, or butter that tastes and smells like the refrigerator in a batch of cookies. Dried fruits should be moist and plump enough for nibbling, spices fresh and lively (toss out the old and bring in the new), butter fresh enough to spread on toast. The best ingredients make the best cookies.

### Baking Powder and Baking Soda
Some cookies are leavened with either baking powder or baking soda or both. Be sure that baking powder is fresh and stored in a well-sealed container. If in doubt, treat yourself to a new tin.

### Butter versus Shortening or Margarine
Butter tastes better than shortening or margarine, and unsalted butter tastes even better. Salted butter contains 1/4 teaspoon of salt per stick (1 teaspoon per pound), which is too much salt for most cookies even if no salt is added in the recipe. Many bakers substitute shortening or margarine for up to half of the butter because these fats produce a lighter, tenderer cookie. I don't.

In my experience, technique makes tenderness: Doughs made exclusively with butter can be exquisitely tender if properly mixed and handled, as I have described in each recipe; superior flavor is the added bonus. If you must use margarine or shortening for all or part of the butter, avoid tub margarines, butter substitutes, and spreads, which may contain a very high percentage of water. These products are not intended for baking; results will be unpredictable. Do not expect predictable results either if you substitute vegetable oils for solid fats.

### Chocolate Chips or Morsels and Bar Chocolate
Chocolate chips are especially formulated for making chocolate chip and other similar cookies—and that is what they are best for—rather than for melting and blending with batter. Chocolate chips do not scorch in a hot oven or when they come in contact with hot cookie sheets; they also retain their smooth soft texture after the cookies have cooled. The brands that I like are Nestlé Toll House, Ghirardelli, and Guittard.

Keep in mind that chocolate chips or morsels are actually sweeter, less smooth, and less chocolatey than regular semisweet or bittersweet chocolate, and they do not melt well. When a recipe calls for several ounces of bittersweet or semisweet chocolate to be melted and blended into brownies or chocolate dough, I always choose a good-quality baking or nibbling chocolate, instead of chocolate chips. The brands that I like are Callebaut, Ghirardelli, Guittard, Lindt, Scharffen Berger, and Valrhona.

### Cocoa
Cocoa powder used for baking is unsweetened and either natural, usually simply labeled "unsweetened cocoa powder," or Dutch process

(alkalized), also called European style. Both types of cocoa are bitter when tasted alone. Of the two, natural cocoa has a fruitier chocolate flavor, which is more acidic and tart; alkalized cocoa has a mellower, almost nutty, toasted chocolate flavor. It is best to use the type of cocoa called for in the recipe, unless you are given a choice. Ghirardelli, Hershey's (brown label), and Nestlé are natural cocoas, which are readily available in the supermarket. Droste's is the best of the Dutch process cocoas widely available in supermarkets. Superb quality cocoas such as Merckens (natural or Dutch process), Valrhona (Dutch process), Pernigotti (Dutch process), Bensdorp (Dutch process), or Van Leer (Dutch process) are available at specialty food stores and by mail order (see page 115).

## Coffee and Espresso

I use instant espresso powder from Medalia d'Oro when espresso powder is called for. To substitute regular instant coffee powder or freeze-dried instant, use 25 to 30 percent more than the recipe calls for. If a recipe calls for freshly ground fresh coffee beans, use freshly roasted beans from a gourmet coffee purveyor, and grind them yourself preferably. Bypass the vacuum-packed can of ground coffee from the supermarket.

## Dried Fruits

These should be moist, plump, and flavorful. Whole pieces are always better, fresher, and moister than prechopped or extruded pellets, even if you have to chop your own. Use an oiled knife or oiled scissors to cut or chop sticky fruit.

## Flour

The recipes in this collection were tested and developed with bleached all-purpose flour. Unbleached flour generally has a higher protein content, which may produce a tougher, browner, flatter cookie.

## Nuts

For freshness and flavor buy nuts raw, rather than toasted, and in bulk from stores that have a lot of turnover, rather than packaged from the supermarket. Larger halves and pieces stay fresher longer; it's better to chop them yourself. Nuts keep well in the freezer, packaged airtight.

Fresh nuts are delicious raw, but toasting brings out such rich new flavors that almonds and hazelnuts are virtually transformed. Toasted nuts are also extra crunchy.

### How to Toast Nuts

To toast nuts spread them in a single layer on an ungreased cookie sheet. Bake in a preheated oven (350°F. for almonds and hazelnuts; 325°F. for pecans and walnuts) for 10 to 20 minutes, depending on the type of nut and whether they are whole, sliced, or slivered. Check the color and flavor of the nuts frequently, and stir to redistribute them on the pan. When chopped toasted nuts are called for, toast them whole or in large pieces, let them cool thoroughly, then chop them.

Almonds and hazelnuts are done when they are golden brown when you bite or cut them in half. To rub the bitter skins from toasted hazelnuts, cool them thoroughly, then rub the nuts together until most of the skins flake off. Pecans and walnuts are done when fragrant and lightly colored.

### How to Grind Nuts

To pulverize or grind nuts in a food processor without making paste or nut butter, start with a perfectly dry processor bowl and blade and nuts at room temperature. (Frozen or cold nuts will produce moisture that turns the nuts to paste, as will nuts still hot from the oven.) Use short pulses, stopping from time to time to scrape the corners of the processor bowl with a skewer or chopstick. If you observe these rules, there is no particular need to add flour or sugar to the nuts to keep them dry, although that is a good precaution.

### Spices and Extracts

For the best and brightest flavors use pure extracts, real ground cinnamon, freshly grated nutmeg, and spices that still smell potent in the bottle.

### Sugar

In recipes with white sugar, I prefer the bright taste of granulated sugar over powdered sugar in almost all cookie recipes.

Professional bakers use sugar with a finer granulation than the regular sugar available in the supermarket. While finer sugar makes cookies lighter and more tender, all of the cookies in this collection were tested with supermarket granulated sugar and all are tender when correctly made. If your local supermarket brand of sugar is coarser than regular salt and/or you think that your cookies could be more tender, switch to superfine or bar sugar, or process your regular granulated sugar briefly in the food processor before using it.

Light (golden) brown and dark brown sugars impart wonderful caramel or butterscotch flavor to cookies. I usually specify my preference for light or dark brown sugar. Brown sugar should be lump free before it is added to a batter or dough; it is unlikely to smooth out after it is added. Soft lumps can be squeezed with your fingers or mashed with a fork before adding. If the brown sugar is quite hard or has hard lumps, process it in the food processor or sift out hard lumps. Warming the sugar to soften it will warm and possibly melt your cookie dough. If in doubt, save hard brown sugar for your oatmeal, to make baked apples or applesauce, or for any recipe that does not require perfect blending with other ingredients before it is baked or cooked. Brown sugar is measured by packing it fairly firmly into the measuring cup.

Maple sugar, also called maple granules, is available in specialty food stores and by mail order. Substitute it for granulated or brown sugar in a simple butter cookie or shortbread for a delicate, if expensive, treat.

Powdered sugar, also called confectioners' sugar or icing sugar, is granulated sugar that has been pulverized and mixed with a little cornstarch to prevent clumping. I use powdered sugar mostly for dusting—sieved over Linzer Cookies or Lemon Bars, for example. I rarely mix it into cookie dough because I do not find the added tenderness that it imparts to cookies worth the dull, uncooked starch flavor and powdery sensation on the palate.

# Equipment

Put away your car keys and credit cards. Simple but successful cookie baking requires simple basic equipment rather than a specialized *batterie de cuisine*. Even a minimally equipped kitchen can turn out good cookies so long as the oven is reliable and the cookie sheets are adequate.

### Bowls

To prevent sugar and flour from flying when beating with a hand-held electric mixer, choose mixing bowls that are relatively tall and deep rather than wide and shallow. The weight of glass or crockery bowls makes them nice and stable, but stainless steel is fine if that is what you have.

### Cookie Sheets and Brownie Pans

Every pan bakes a little differently, depending on the material, thickness, weight, and surface reflection. If your oven temperature is accurate but cookies, brownies, and bars bake unevenly or brown too quickly on the bottom and edges, your pans may be too thin or too dark. Parchment paper liners might help promote even baking, or try two thin pans, one on top of the other, to simulate air-cushioned pans, for extra insulation.

When buying new pans, look for medium- to heavy-weight pans. Baking sheets should be rimless or with low rims. Light-colored, shiny, or at least somewhat reflective metal surfaces work better than dark or dull ones. Air-cushioned baking sheets bake quite evenly, but they may take a little longer than the time given in most recipes; they are better for soft or chewy cookies rather than crisp ones. All of the cookies and brownies in this collection were tested with medium-weight aluminum pans. Cookie sheets were 16 X 12-inch half sheet pans with 1-inch rims on all four sides.

### Cooling Racks

Simple and inexpensive from the hardware store, or fancy and French, it doesn't really matter so long as you have some kind of rack or grid with lots of air circulation that cookies can cool quickly on.

### Mixers and Spoons

Most of the recipes in this book call for a moderate amount of mixing, rather than lengthy beating. Unless specified otherwise, a hand-held mixer or a big wooden or metal spoon is the best mixing tool for single batches of cookies and may actually prevent overmixing as compared with bigger, more powerful heavy-duty electric stand mixers. If you double or triple recipes, a heavy-duty stand mixer will be needed, in combination with restraint, where necessary, to avoid overmixing.

### Pancake Turner

Removing individual cookies from baking sheets is easiest to do with an ordinary kitchen pancake turner/spatula. Choose the thin metal kind; plastic or Teflon-coated ones are thicker and harder to slip under cookies.

### Portion or Cookie Scoops

Nonessential but wonderful—the fast and easy way to make lots of evenly sized drop cookies, or balls of dough in specific sizes, even when the dough or batter is stiff or chilled. The scoops work like ice cream scoops: A squeeze of the handle releases the contents. These are found in better cookware stores and in restaurant supply stores (for the largest selection), where they are called portion scoops, or dishers, or food servers. Brands are Vollrath, Hamilton Beach, and Stöckel (which is the same as Intedge Bright Knight). The most useful sizes are #100 (2 level teaspoons to form a 1-inch ball), #60 (slightly more than a level tablespoon to form a 1 1/4-inch ball), and #30 (2 tablespoons to form a 1 1/2-inch ball).

### Rolling Pins

I roll cookie dough between sheets of plastic or wax paper, so my only requirement is a rolling pin that is straight rather than tapered. Cooks always have personal preferences when it comes to rolling pins: large and heavy or small and light, with or without handles. Use what is comfortable for you. Improvisational items, such as tall bottles, thick pieces of dowel, or lengths of pipe, make adequate rolling pins as well.

### Thermometers

An oven thermometer is useful for checking the accuracy of your oven dial. An instant-read thermometer is essential if you plan to temper chocolate for dipping cookies. Both are available in the housewares department of hardware stores or in kitchen specialty shops and by mail order.

### Timer

Cookies are easily overbaked if left in the oven a minute or two longer than necessary. A timer that rings or buzzes keeps the busy or distracted cook from forgetting the cookies in the oven.

### Whisks

Wire whisks are not essential for cookie bakers, but they are superb for blending dry ingredients together and fluffing up the flour in lieu of sifting, and, in general, for whisking things together.

# Resources

## Mail Order and Retail Sources

### Sur La Table
1765 Sixth Ave. S.
Seattle, WA 98134-1608
1-800-243-0852
Retail stores on the West Coast and mail order catalogue.

*All kinds of tools and equipment, cookie cutters, decorations, gold leaf and gold powder, cookie sheets, silicon sheets, Scharffen Berger and Valrhona chocolates.*

### Williams-Sonoma
POB 7456
San Francisco, CA 94120-7456
1-800-541-2233
Retail stores across the country and mail order catalogue.

*All kinds of tools and equipment, Pernigotti cocoa, Valrhona and Callebaut chocolates.*

### King Arthur Flour
### The Baker's Catalogue
POB 876
Norwich, VT 05055-0876
1-800-827-6836

*Everything for the baker. Merckens and Van Leer cocoas, various chocolates, coarse white and colored sugar crystals, and a vast selection of other cookie decorations, maple granules, crystallized ginger, gold leaf and gold powder.*

### Parrish's Cake Decorating Supply, Inc.
225 West 146 St.
Gardena, CA 90248
1-800-736-8443
Retail store and mail order catalogue.

*Everything for the cookie maker and decorator.*

### Sweet Celebrations
### (Maid of Scandinavia)
7009 Washington Ave. S.
Edina, MN 55439
1-800-328-6722

*Everything for the cookie maker and decorator, including candy coat colors appropriate for coloring white chocolate.*

### Dean & Deluca
560 Broadway
New York, NY 10012
1-800-227-7714
Retail stores and mail order catalogue.

*Ingredients and equipment.*

*Don't forget local natural foods and health food stores for nuts, dried fruits, organic flour, unsweetened coconut, and spices.*

# Index

Almond(s)
  Biscotti, 82–83
  Chewy Cherry Bars, 104
  Crust for Apricot Bars, 103
  Macaroons, 64
  Mandelbrodt, 85
  Orange Biscotti, 83
  toasting method, 111
  Toffee Bars, 108
Apricot(s)
  Lemon Bars, 102–3
  Nut Bars, 105
  Nut Rugelach, 71

baking powder/soda, 110
baking tips, 10–14
  Steve Ritual, 94
  test batch, 61
bar chocolate, 45, 110
  melting, 14–15
  tempering, 17–19
Bars, 90–91, 100–109
  Apricot-Lemon, 102–3
  Blondies, 100
  Chewy Almond and Cherry, 104
  Fruit and Nut, 105
  Lemon, 101
  pans, 113
  preparation tips, 91
  Rocky Road, 106–7
  Toffee, 108
  Turtle, 109
  variations, 103
  *See also* Brownies
Basic Butter Cookies, 30–32
  chocolate-dipped, 17

filled sandwiches, 19, 20
variations, 32
Basic Shortbread, 24–25
Beacon Hill Cookies, 57
beading, 15–16
Biscotti, 80–89
  Almond, 82–83
  Chocolate, 89
  chocolate-dipped, 17
  Cornmeal and Fruit, 84
  Mandelbrodt, 85
  Orange-Chocolate Chip, 86–87
  preparation tips, 81
  variations, 81, 83, 87, 89
Bittersweet/Semisweet Chocolate
  Beacon Hill Cookies, 57
  Brownies, 96
  Chocolate Decadence Cookies, 52
  Chocolate Ganache, 21
  cookies dipped in, 17, 62
  melting, 15
  *See also* Chocolate Chip(s)
Blondies, 100
Bourbon Pecan Shortbread, 25
Bovine Bakery, 76
bowls, 113
Brown Sugar, 112
Bridget's Oat-Raisin-Coconut
  Cookies, 76
Bromberg, Eric and Bruce, 85
Brownies, 90–100
  Bittersweet, 96
  Blondies, 100
  Espresso Swirl, 98–99
  New Classic, 92–95
  pans, 113

  preparation tips, 91, 94
  Very Fudgey, 97
Brown Sugar, 112
  Butter Cookies, 32
    dipped in white chocolate, 1?
    filled sandwiches, 19, 20
  Shortbread, 25
butter
  melted, 48, 75
  shortening or margarine vs., 110
  softened, 10
Butter Cookies, 28–43
  Basic, 30–32
  Espresso Walnut, 35–36
  filled sandwiches, 19, 20
  impressions, 14
  Linzer, 37–39
  Mexican Wedding Cakes, 40–42
  preparation tips, 29
  Snicker Doodles, 43
  storage, 12
  Vanilla Sugar, 33–34
  variations, 17, 32, 39, 42
Butter Pecan Cookies, 32
  dipped in white chocolate, 17
  white chocolate–filled
    sandwiches, 19

Cardamom Shortbread, 25
Cashew Cookies, 74
Chewy Almond and Cherry Bars, 10?
chilling and resting dough, 12–13
  Double Chocolate Chip
    Cookies, 50, 51
  Oatmeal Cookie, 75
  Peanut Butter Cookies, 72

colate
iscotti, 89
decadence Cookies, 52–53
ipped cookies, 17
spresso Wafers, 59
lling, 19–20
Ganache, 21
melting method, 14–15
Orange Biscotti, 89
iping, 14
ecommended brands, 110
Shortbread, 26–27
empering, 17–19
Wafers, 58–59
See also Brownies; Chocolate
    Cookies; specific types
ocolate Chip(s), 45, 110
Biscotti, 83, 87
Blondies, 100
Chocolate Decadence Cookies, 52
Chocolate-Hazelnut Meringue
    Kisses, 46
Chocolate-Hazelnut Rugelach, 71
cookies and variations, 48–51
Faux Florentines, 47
Mocha Biscotti, 89
Orange Biscotti, 86–87
recommended brands, 110
Rocky Road Bars, 107
Toffee Bars, 108
ocolate Chip Cookie, 48–49
Double Chocolate Chip, 50–51
ice cream–filled sandwiches, 20
variations, 49
ocolate Cookies, 44–59
baking tips, 45

Beacon Hill, 57
Chocolate Chip, 48–49
Chocolate Decadence, 52–53
Double Chocolate Chip, 50–51
Faux Florentines, 47
Hazelnut Meringue Kisses, 46
Macadamia and White
    Chocolate Chunk, 56
Robert's, 54–55
variations, 46, 49, 51, 59
Wafers, 58–59
Chocolate Ganache, 21, 73
Chocolate-Hazelnut
    Biscotti, 89
    Meringue Kisses, 46
    Rugelach, 71
Cinnamon
    Moravian Spice Cookies, 77
    Rugelach, 70
    Snicker Doodles, 43
    Spicy Chocolate-Pecan Cookies, 51
Classic Cookies. See Cookie Classics
Cocoa
    Chocolate Biscotti, 89
    Chocolate Wafers, 58–59
    Double Chocolate Chip
        Cookies, 50–51
    recommended powders, 110–11
    Very Fudgey Brownies, 97
Coconut
    Macaroons, 62–63
    Oat-Raisin Cookies, 76
    Sticks, 65
Coffee, 111
    Chocolate Biscotti, 89
    Chocolate Espresso Wafers, 59

Double Chocolate Mocha
    Cookies, 51
Espresso Swirl Brownies, 98–99
Espresso Walnut Cookies, 35–36
Mocha Latte/Mocha Espresso
    Biscotti, 89
Mocha-Nut Meringue Kisses, 46
Mocha Shortbread, 26
Robert's Chocolate Cookies, 54–55
colored sprinkles, 15–16
confectioners' sugar, 112
Cookie Classics, 60–79
    Almond Macaroons, 64
    Cashew Cookies, 74
    Coconut Macaroons, 62–63
    Coconut Sticks, 65
    Ginger Snaps, 78–79
    Lemon Ginger Wafers, 66–67
    Maya's Lemon Wafers, 68–69
    Moravian Spice Cookies, 77
    Oatmeal Cookies, 75
    Oat-Raisin-Coconut Cookies, 76
    Peanut Butter Cookies, 72–73
    preparation tips, 61
    Rugelach, 70–71
    variations, 69, 71, 73
cookie scoop, 13, 14
    recommended brands, 114
cookie sheets and pans, 113
    baking tips, 10–12
    cooling between batches, 10
    liners, 10–11, 91
    preparing, 12
cooling process, 10, 11–12
cooling racks, 113
Cornmeal and Fruit Biscotti, 84

Cunningham, Marion, 92
cutting/shaping cookies, 13–14, 61

dark brown sugar, 112
Date(s)
  Nut Bars, 105
  Nut Rugelach, 71
David, Narsai, 52
decorating techniques, 14–19
dipping in chocolate, 17
Double Chocolate Chip Cookes, 50–51
  ice cream-filled sandwiches, 20
  variations, 51
Double Chocolate Cookies, 51
Double Chocolate Mint Cookies, 52
Double Chocolate Mocha Cookies, 51
dough
  adding flour to, 9–10
  chilling and resting, 12–13
  freezing, 13
  kneading, 9–10
  rolling and cutting, 13–14
  scooping and shaping, 14
dried fruits, 111
  Chewy Almond Bars, 104
  Cornmeal Biscotti, 84
  Nut Bars, 105
dry measures, 9

Easy Cookie Icing, 15
Eggnog Cookies, 32
equipment, 113–14
Espresso, 111
  Mocha Biscotti, 89
  Swirl Brownies, 98–99
  Walnut Cookies, 35–36

Extra Bittersweet Scharffen
  Berger Brownies, 96
extracts, use of fresh, 112

Faux Florentines, 47
Filled Cookies
  Rugelach, 70–71
  sandwich, 19–21
  storage, 12
  *See also* Thumbprints
flocking, 15–16
Florentines, Faux, 47
flour, 111
  adding to batter, 9–10
  aerating, 10
  best choice, 8, 111
  measuring, 9
  mixing, 10
  Wondra, 85
foil pan lining, 10–11, 91
food colorings, 15
Fruit and Nut Bars, 105

Ganache, Chocolate, 21
Ginger
  Lemon Wafers, 66–67
  Moravian Spice Cookies, 77
  Snaps, 78–79
gold powder, 17

Hazelnut(s)
  Biscotti, 83
  Chocolate Biscotti, 89
  Chocolate Meringue Kisses, 46
  Chocolate Rugelach, 71
  Crust for Apricot Bars, 103

Nut Clusters, 49
  toasting method, 111–12

icing, 15
impressions, 14, 73
ingredient choices, 110–12

Jungle Jim's, 82

Klein, Maya, 68, 94
Klein, Steve, 94

Lemon(s)
  Apricot Bars, 102–3
  Bars, 101
  Curd, 20
  Ginger Wafers, 66–67
  Maya's Wafers, 68–69
  Poppy Seed Wafers, 69
Lewis, Edna, 77
light (golden) brown sugar, 112
liners, 10, 11–12
Linzer Cookies, 37–39
  variation, 39
liquid measures, 9
Lower-Fat
  Chocolate Wafers, 58–59
  Meringue Kisses, 46
  Orange-Chocolate Chip
    Biscotti, 87
  Very Fudgey Brownies, 97
lustre dust, 17

Macadamia(s)
  Nut Clusters, 49
  White Chocolate Chunk Cookies,

aroons
mond, 64
ocolate-dipped, 17
oconut, 62–63
delbrodt, 85
le Butter Cookies, 32
le sugar, 112
garine, butter vs., 110
th'a Tender Mandelbrodt, 85
ya's Lemon Wafers, 68–69
ariations, 69
asurement tips, 8–9
ted butter
asic Shortbread, 23
hocolate Chip Cookies, 48
atmeal Cookies, 75
eanut Butter Cookies, 72
ted chocolate, 14–17
ecorating with, 15–16
elting method, 14–15
s Sandwich Cookie filling, 20
empered, 17–19
ringues, 46
xican Chocolate Wafers, 59
hocolate-filled sandwiches, 20
xican Wedding Cakes, 40–42
ariation, 42
k chocolate
elting, 14–15
ocky Road Bars, 107
empering temperature, 19
offee Bars, 108
urtle Bars, 109
ni Peanut Butter Cookies, 73
nt
Chocolate Wafers, 59

Double Chocolate Cookies, 52
mixers, electric, 114
mixing procedure, 9–10
Mocha
    Double Chocolate Cookies, 51
    Espresso Biscotti, 89
    Nut Meringue Kisses, 46
    Shortbread, 26
Moravian Spice Cookies, 77

New Classic Brownies, 92–95
    Espresso Swirl Brownies, 98–99
Nut(s), 111
    Clusters, 49
    Crust for Apricot Bars, 103
    Fruit Bars, 105
    grinding, 112
    Thumbprints, 42
    toasting, 111–12
    *See also specific kinds*
Nutmeg Shortbread, 25
Nutty Thumbprint Cookies, 42
    Chocolate Ganache filling, 21

Oatmeal
    Cookies, 75
    Faux Florentines, 47
oats, rolled
    Macadamia and White Chocolate
        Chunk Cookies, 56
    Oatmeal Cookies, 75
    Raisin-Coconut Cookies, 76
Orange(s)
    Almond Biscotti, 83
    Chocolate Biscotti, 89
    Chocolate Chip Biscotti, 86–87

oven
    cookie sheet positioning, 10
    preheating, 10
    thermometer, 10, 114

pancake turner, 12, 114
pans. *See* cookie sheets and pans
parchment paper, 10, 11, 45
Peanut(s)
    Filling, 21
    Shortbread, 25
Peanut Butter
    Cookies, 72–73
    Filling, 20–21
    Thumbprints, 73
    variations, 73
Pecan(s)
    Chocolate Chip Cookies, 48
    Chocolate Decadence Cookies, 52
    New Classic Brownies, 93–94
    Spicy Chocolate Cookies, 51
    toasting method, 111, 112
    Turtle Bars, 109
petal dust, 17
piping, 14
portion scoops, 13, 14, 114
powdered sugar, 12, 112
    Easy Cookie Icing, 15
    Mexican Wedding Cakes, 40–42

Radin, Beryl, 109
Raisin(s)
    Cornmeal Biscotti, 84
    Oat-Coconut Cookies, 76
    Robert's Chocolate Cookies, 54–55
    Rocky Road Bars, 106–7

rolling out method, 8, 13
rolling pins, 114
Rugelach, 70–71
   variations, 71

Sandwich Cookies, 19–21
   fillings, 19–21
   *See also* Thumbprints
Scharffen Berger Chocolate
      Maker, 110
   Extra Bittersweet Brownies, 96
   Robert's Chocolate Cookies, 54–55
scoops, 13, 14, 114
semisweet chocolate. *See*
   Bittersweet/Semisweet
   Chocolate; Chocolate Chip(s)
Shortbread, 22–27
   Basic, 24–25
   Chocolate, 26–27
   preparation tips, 22, 24
   storage, 12
   variations, 25, 26
shortening, butter vs., 110
silver powder, 17
Snicker Doodles, 43
spices
   Moravian Cookies, 77
   Shortbread variations, 25
   use of fresh, 61, 112
Spicy Chocolate-Pecan Cookies, 51
Spicy Chocolate Shortbread, 26
spoons, 114
Steinberg, Robert, 54
Steve Ritual (brownie baking), 95
storing cookies, 12, 17
sugar, 8, 112

Sugar Cookies, 33–34
superfine sugar, 8

tempered chocolate, 17–19
   method, 18–19
tender cookies, tips for making, 8
test baking, 61
thermometers, 10, 114
Thumbprints
   fillings, 20–21
   Lemon Curd, 20
   Linzer, 39
   Nutty, 42
   Peanut Butter, 73
   storage, 12
   variations, 39
Tibone, Carole, 82
timers, 114
tinting, 15
toasting nuts, 111–12
Toffee Bars, 108
Turtle Bars, 109

unsweetened chocolate
   Bittersweet Brownies, 96
   New Classic Brownies, 92–95
   Robert's Chocolate Cookies, 54–55

Vanilla Sugar Cookies, 33–34
   filled sandwiches, 19, 20
Very Fudgey Brownies, 97

Wafers
   Chocolate, 58–59
   filled sandwiches, 20
   Lemon Ginger, 66–67

   Maya's Lemon, 68–69
Walnut(s)
   Beacon Hill Cookies, 57
   Blondies, 100
   Chocolate Biscotti, 89
   Chocolate Chip Biscotti, 83, 87
   Chocolate Chip Cookies, 48
   Chocolate Decadence Cookies
   Double Chocolate Chip Cookies
   Espresso Cookies, 35–36
   Fruit and Nut Bars, 105
   New Classic Brownies, 93–94
   Robert's Chocolate Cookies, 54
   Rocky Road Bars, 107
   Rugelach, 70–71
   Shortbread, 25
   toasting method, 111, 112
whisks, 114
White Chocolate
   for dipping, 17
   Macadamia Chocolate Chunk
      Cookies, 56
   melting, 15
   tempering temperature, 19
Wondra flour, 85